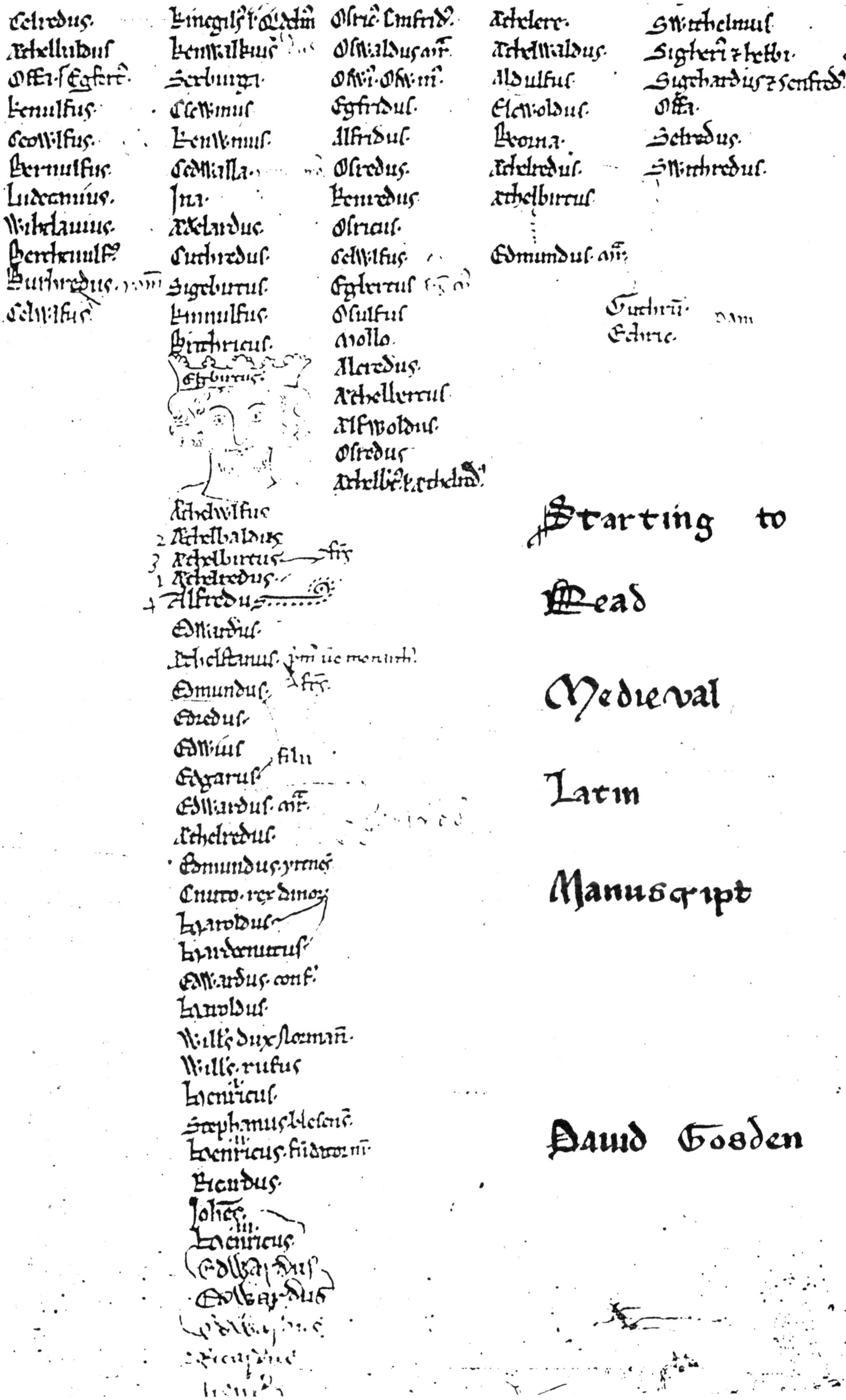

Starting to Read Medieval Latin Manuscript

David Gosden

STARTING TO READ MEDIEVAL LATIN MANUSCRIPT

AN INTRODUTION FOR STUDENTS
OF MEDIEVAL HISTORY
AND GENEALOGY
WHO WISH TO VENTURE
INTO LATIN TEXTS

DAVID GOSDEN

Students who know no Latin are advised that this book assumes some acquaintance with Latin. The ideal first step for such students is to use E.A. Gooder's *"Latin for Local History"* (Longmans).

First published in 1993 by **Llanerch Publishers.**

ISBN **1 897853 22 1**

Introduction

My desire to pass on the skills developed in this book arose from some years of acquiring them myself - the hard way. At that time there did not seem to be a book such as this, nor do I know of one now, and I hope this will supply the need.

This book sets out to help the novice reader of medieval Latin manuscripts who has no access to a live teacher and for whom the standard works take too much for granted. The skills and habits you will need are best picked up, apprentice-wise, in the company of an experienced reader. I have tried to provide a comparable experience, sharing with you the kind of thinking and guidance that ideally you would receive from the lips of such a master of the trade. This book should be read in that spirit.

The vast quantity of surviving Latin manuscripts exhibits a wide variety of scribal hands, not surprisingly. This introduction to the skills of reading medieval Latin MSS can only sample a few hands, chosen for their usefulness, not as representatives. When you have mastered these, you will be in a position to tackle a wider range, referring when necessary to handbooks such as Hector's and Iredale's (see "Further Reading").

Although the chapters deal with identifiable topics, they cannot be taken out of sequence, except possibly those marked with an asterisk in the table of Contents as being relatively free-floating. The material is introduced in a carefully planned progression, and later chapters assume that you have read the earlier chapters.

At various points I invite you to carry out some sort of exercise. You are strongly urged to take these opportunities[1]. Like all teach-yourself books, this volume will lose in effectiveness if you try to rush through it. A Key provides answers to exercises; it also contains transcriptions of quotations and examples that are not discussed in detail.

I make certain assumptions about the extent of your knowledge before you start on this particular study. You will need a fair grasp of traditional Latin grammar. You may not feel that you can recall your school Latin, but it probably suffices if you have at some time studied Latin up to about fourth-year level in a secondary school. It will come back to you. Those with no Latin will find E.A.Gooder's <u>Latin for Local History</u> invaluable.

Vocabulary is a different matter. The material I shall bring before you employs a very simple vocabulary. Much of it is post-classical, not found in dictionaries of classical Latin. For this you have at least three sources of help: Appendix C provides the meanings of the commonest post-classical words needed for this book; early in Chapter One I offer you a plainly printed text similar in content to the main text you will study; and there are books..... But they demand careful consideration.

The <u>Revised Medieval Latin Word-List from British and Irish Sources</u>, prepared by R.E.Latham and published for the British Academy by The Oxford University Press (1965)[2] is unquestionably the book to obtain. If you expect to practise the craft my book sets out to teach, a copy of Latham's book is indispensable. It demands patience and skill in use, as does any

---

1. A hand in the margin indicates opportunities for written practice; a face indicates "mental" rather than written exercises.
2. Reissued 1980 with appendices of corrigenda and addenda.

serious book of reference, but it stands alone. It was designed as a means of preparing a full-scale dictionary. This definitive work[1] is gradually appearing, but it is expensive, and far from complete. Latham's one-volume Word-List can be bought.

A once popular reference source in the field of medieval Latin has now reappeared in facsimile, The Record Interpreter by Charles Trice Martin[2]. I think it unwise at this stage of your study to purchase a copy of Trice Martin. A great deal of research has been done since it appeared. However, if you happen to have access to a copy, you may well find useful the various lists of Latin names. David Iredale's Introduction to the facsimile edition is very helpful.

It is useful to have handy a conventional dictionary of classical Latin for the occasions when your memory fails you.

If you are whole-hearted in your use of this book, you will need one or two practical aids. The exercises already referred to rather lack point unless you have a pen with a broad nib. You also need access to a copying machine. This is one book where you are asked to make photo-copies, not forbidden to do so. If your eyesight is past its peak, you may find a magnifying glass useful occasionally.

Any unattributed page references you meet are to pages of this book itself, but plain line references (e.g."line 18" or "1.18") are to the main teaching text, printed on page 7 and also just before the end papers. This copy of the text is designed to be opened out and so available for consultation as you read other pages. The actual quotations are generally reproductions from the manuscript, but at various points I have had reason to cite passages in transcribed form. There is an index of words cited in MS form

Because my emphasis is on skills and habits, I have not presented very formally, as I proceed, the information that accrues concerning the various signs or marks of abbreviation. You will find a summary of this information at the end, and the books listed under Further Reading contain their own accounts of these signs. Also at the end of the book you will find, listed chapter by chapter, what may be regarded as the main lessons to be learnt, - of all kinds.

Finally, may I offer you a brief glossary of terms that I shall use? They are not at all obscure, but preliminary clarification will save any doubt later on.

ABBREVIATE - to represent a word in writing in such a way that it occupies a smaller portion of the line than the normal or full version would take[3]. This may be achieved by leaving letters out or by using a single sign to represent several letters. It is a general term; particular forms or patterns of abbreviation are explained in the book, in due course.[4] I use SHORTEN as

1. R.E.Latham and others, Dictionary of Medieval Latin from British Sources (Oxford, for the British Academy, A-B 1975, C 1981, D-E 1986).
2. Phillimore, 1982
3. This long, formal definition is necessary because scribes often provided helpful clues above (or below) the abbreviated word. So their aim was not to save time, nor to save ink, but to make best use of expensive parchment.
4. page 42.

an alternative term to express the same meaning.

HAND or SCRIBAL HAND - the particular handwriting of a particular text, presumably but not indisputably the work of a single scribe.

MANUSCRIPT - (i) a handwritten text
(ii) handwriting

MEDIEVAL - a term variously used and spelt! I follow Latham in the latter respect. The term "medieval" refers to Latin documents dating roughly from the Saxon period to the final triumph of the printing press. However, this Introductory book concentrates on hands from one rich period of medieval Latin documents.

PALAEOGRAPHY - (note the spelling) is strictly the whole, diverse discipline centred on the interpretation, date and distribution of old handwritten documents, but the term is sometimes used for the foundation of it all, learning to read them.

SCRIPT - among the various uses of this word, note its meaning as the model to which a scribe aspired as he wrote in his own HAND, i.e. one of the families to which individual HANDS may be assigned. (See the books listed in Further Reading.)

SHORTEN - to abbreviate (q.v.)

TEXT - any defined piece of written or printed language, the defined piece often serving as the basis for discussion etc.

TRANSCRIBE - not simply to copy, but to attempt to reproduce a document in modern form, as closely as possible to the original.

TRANSCRIPT - the product of the act of transcribing.

TRANSCRIPTION - (i) a transcript
(ii) the act (or process) of transcribing.

TRANSLATE - as always, to convey the meaning of a text into some language other than the one it was written in.

CONTENTS

* Asterisks mark "free-floating" chapters (see Introduction)

STARTING TO READ MEDIEVAL LATIN MANUSCRIPT

On Making Things Easy For Yourself

What do you make of this?

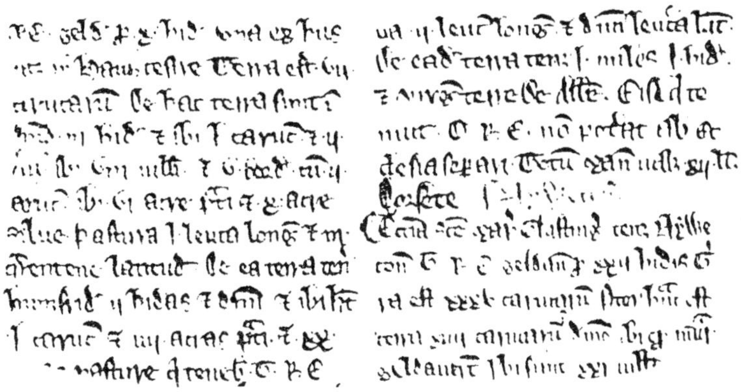

Text I

Do not be alarmed! This little piece of text is not for you to decipher now. It is offered as a sample of the difficulties that do arise from time to time and as a sample of the material that makes the skill of the palaeographer seem so remarkable.

Doubtless every advanced skill or expertise is apt to develop around it a certain mystique, and it is easy to see why a famous French expert mnay years ago insisted that the business of deciphering old documents is an "art". Of course reading old Latin texts can be difficult, even for the skilled. Medieval manuscripts were not always models of calligraphy, nor are they all in a good state of repair. Nevertheless, there is no need for beginners to make things unnecessarily difficult for themselves. I hope in this little book to show ways in which the novice can progress by easy stages, following, as far as possible, the time-honoured principle of working from the known to the unknown.

The little sample of manuscript is particularly nasty, not least because the ink is faint and the letters are tiny. Modern technology can help with the latter problem, as with this example:

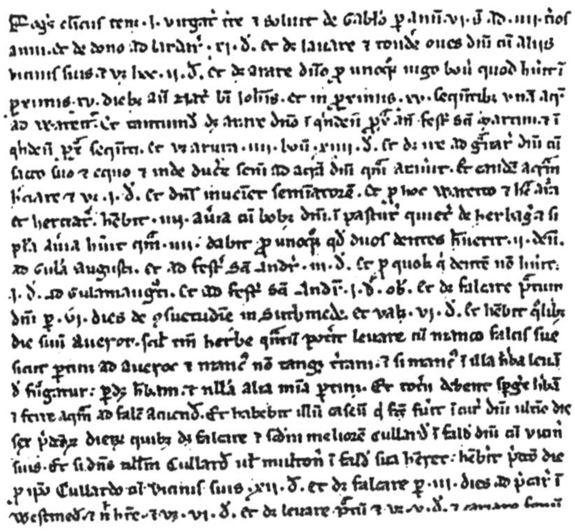

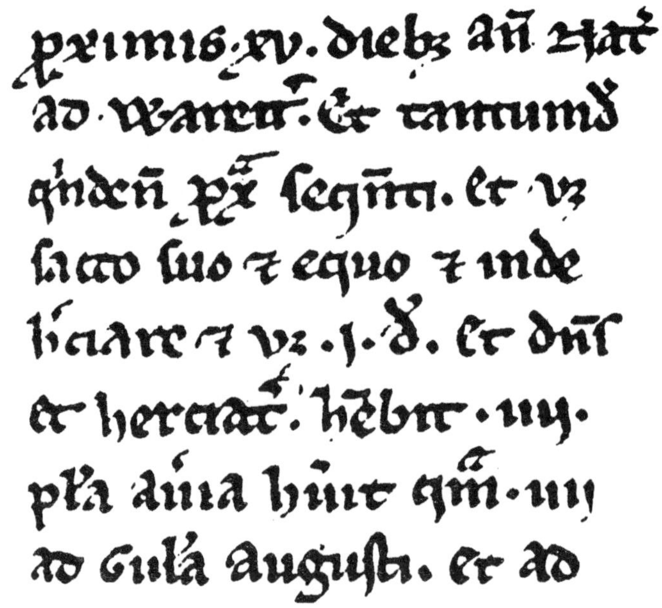

Text II

Difficulties do not reside solely in the appearance of a medieval text. The content may also present problems. There may be a high proportion of place-names and personal names, totally unlike the Latin of the main text, adorned with capital letters (always trickier to interpret) and likely to be spelled inconsistently:

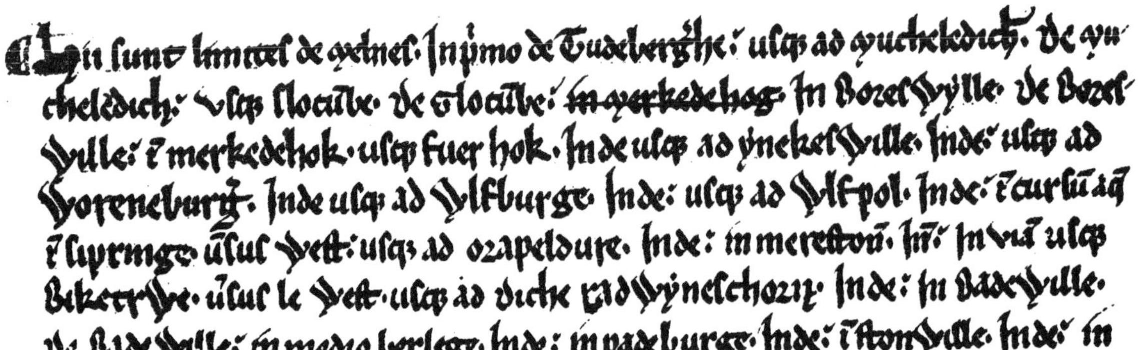

Text III

Here is a partial transcription of that text, preserving the abbreviated forms of words, to illustrate the problems of names.

Hii sunt limites de melnes. Inp^{i}mo de Tudeberg'he usq' ad mucheledich'. De mucheledich usq' slocu'be. De Slocu'be in merkedehog [the last two words deleted] in Boreswylle. De Boreswille i' merkedehok usq' Fuerhok. Inde usq' ad ynekeswille. Inde usq' ad Woreneburg. Inde usq' ad Wlfburge. Inde usq' ad Wlfpol. Inde i' cursum aque i' sipringe v'sus West usq' ad orapeldure. Inde in mereston'. In' in via' usq' Biketrwe v'sus le West usq' ad Diche radwyneschorn'. Inde in Badewille. De Badewille in medio berlege. Inde in padeburge. Inde i' stonwille. Inde in....

In any case, beginners may well not be familiar with the kind of Latin found in historical documents. Specialist vocabulary and non-classical syntax can trap the unwary. Indeed, different kinds of document have very distinctive kinds of language, and the novice is not helped by too rapid a tour through a great variety of texts.

When tackling a new scribal hand, now and later, unskilled readers should improve their chances by first studying a printed transcript of material that they know to be similar in kind, as regards content or subject-matter. Even a translation into English would be better than nothing. You are not cheating if you approach a manuscript with some idea of what it might say, provided that you use this insight as a means of learning to interpret the idiosyncrasies of your scribe, not as a means of by-passing them. This approach is widely recommended.

The main examples used in this beginners' Guide are from an unpublished manorial survey of the mid-thirteenth century. To help you, I could offer now some material concerning the same manor, indeed, the same individual tenant, from a survey conducted about twenty years previously. That might be too helpful. As a compromise, therefore, we offer you a transcript of material from a manor not far from the source of our main text.[1] In case your Latin is shaky I provide a translation on this occasion. But the printed transcript is the key.

1. You will find a copy of the original manuscript in Appendix A.

Redditus et Servicia Villanorum

1. Willelmus Avenel tenet j virgatam terre et reddet[sic plene] in gabulo per annum iiij s. scilicet ad quemlibet terminum
2. xij d. et ad lardarium ad Natale xij d. Et debet adiuvare ad lavandos et tondendos
3. oves domini et valet hoc ij d. et debet warectare ad Festum Sancti Johannis Baptiste pro viij bobus
4. vij acras vel si pauciores boves habuerit waractabit pro unoquoque bove quem habuerit octavam
5. partem vij acrarum. Et tantumdem debet arare domino statim post Festum Beati Martini, et
6. valet hec arura si octo boves habuerit v s. x d. et pro hac arura debet habere boves suos cum bobus
7. domini in pastura domini, et debet sarclare bladum domini una die in estate cum j homine usque no-
8. nam, et si dominus illum pascet usque vesperam, et valet hoc ob., et debet falcare pratum domini per
9. ij dies et dominus illum pascet bis in die cum pane de frumento et caseo et valet eius falcatio vj d.
10. et debet levare ad custum suum quantum falcaverit, et valet hoc viij d. et debet cariare pre-
11. dictum fenum in curiam domini et valet cariatio vij d. ob., et debet metere bladum domini ad preces
12. per iij dies in autumpno cum ij hominibus et dominus illos pascet bis in die, scilicet, premissis ij
13. diebus cum pane et caseo et tertia die in pane et caseo ad nonam et sero in pane, carne et cervisio
14. in curia domini, et quarta die si opus fuerit debet metere cum j homine et dominus illum pascet et valet mes-
15. sio sua xiiij d., et debet cariare bladum domini et nil habere et valet cariacio eius ij s. et debet sum-
16. magiare corredium domini de burgo quociens opus fuerit et valet quelibet cariacio ij d. et
17. debet cariare buscam ad curiam contra adventum domini et valet quelibet cariacio ij d. et debet venire
18. bis in anno ad preces domini cum bobus suis, et valet arura eiusdem viij d. si viij boves habeat,
19. et debet cariare victualia domini ad pontem de Stan', et valet hoc x d. et debet cariare la-
20. nam et caseum domini ubi necesse fuerit in eodem comitatu, vel apud Wynterburn' vel apud Merle-
21. berg', et valet hoc j d.ob.

From British Library Add MS 17450 fol.[172]170r (Ashbury)

Text IV[1]

---

1. In case you decide to attempt a translation of this text, I provide in Appendix B a literal translation with which to compare your version. However, it is the transcription above that matters, typifying the sort

The approach we are using here will be equally appropriate, in general, if you prefer to apply its principles to a text of your own choosing. For clarity's sake I shall proceed on the assumption that you are using my material. In either case, there are useful points to bear in mind.

If at all possible, work from a photographic reproduction of the text[1], but make a fresh copy of it, so that you can mark it with useful memoranda, with impunity.

Begin by marking against each line of the photocopy a line number, so that you can easily find your place. Likewise, lay out your transcript on a line-by-line basis, similarly numbered, for cross-reference, like this:

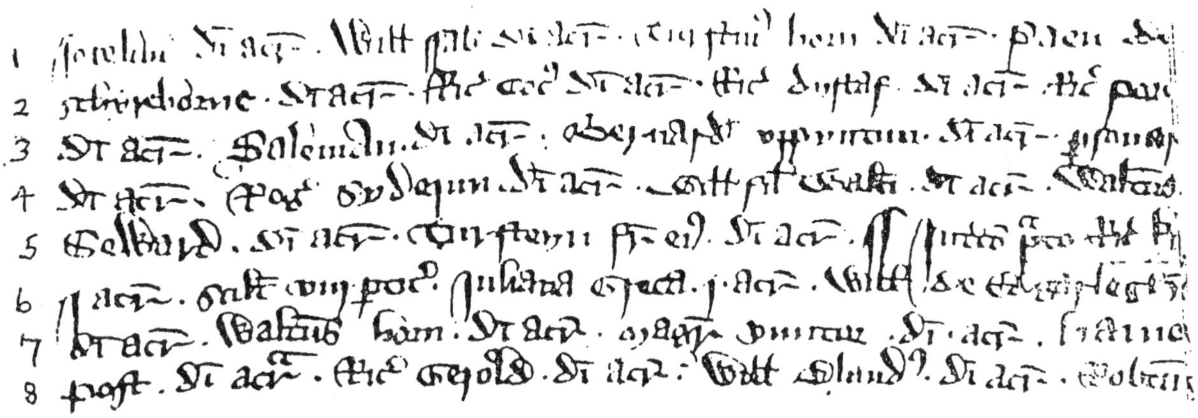

Text V (manuscript)

117 1. Jocelini dimidiam acram. Willelm[illegible] Faber dimidiam acram. [illegible]
acram. [illegible]

2. Schyreborne dimidiam acram, Ricardus Cocus dimidiam acram. Ricardus [illegible] dim- Dys[illegible]
-idium acram. Ricardus Por[illegible] | Uppyntun

3 dimidiam acram. Saleman dimidium acram. Bernard [illegible] dimidiam acram Persona

4. dimidiam acram. Rogerus Syderun dimidiam acram Gill filius Walteri dimidiam acram. Walterus

5 Seward dimidium acram Turstenus frater eius dimidium acram. [illegible] prato
Ricardus K[illegible] In tercio

6. j acram. Scilicet viij pertic'. Iuliana Greca j acram. Willelmus de Edgarlegh [illegible]

7. dimidiam acram. Walterus Horn dimidiam acram. Magister Vinctor dimidiam acram. Hamo

Text V (transcript)

---

1. Many medievam MSS have been microfilmed, and prints can often be derived from this medium, after suitable permission has been obtained.

Treat all encounters with manuscript texts as opportunites for learning, not as tests to see how you have progressed.

Above all, use the manuscript text in front of you as your reference book (not some learned publication, not even this book) until you are sure you have exhausted its possibilities as a guide. This advice is based on the fact that every scribal hand is to some extent unique. Books can only give general information (kinds and periods of script), and leave you with the very tricky problems of assigning your particular sample to one of them and of allowing for individual deviations.

Whole Words And What To Do About Them

Even readers who have heard about the scribal fondness for shortening words may be unprepared for the extent of this practice. They may also be surprised at the degree of difficulty initially presented by it. Mercifully, the great majority of hands include a sprinkling of whole words, and as these are much easier to interpret we begin by simply locating some on a page of text. Be bold! Make a photocopy of Text VI (preferably enlarged), go through it carefully, and ring clearly round any likely whole words. Don't worry about finding them all. Pick out those that you can.

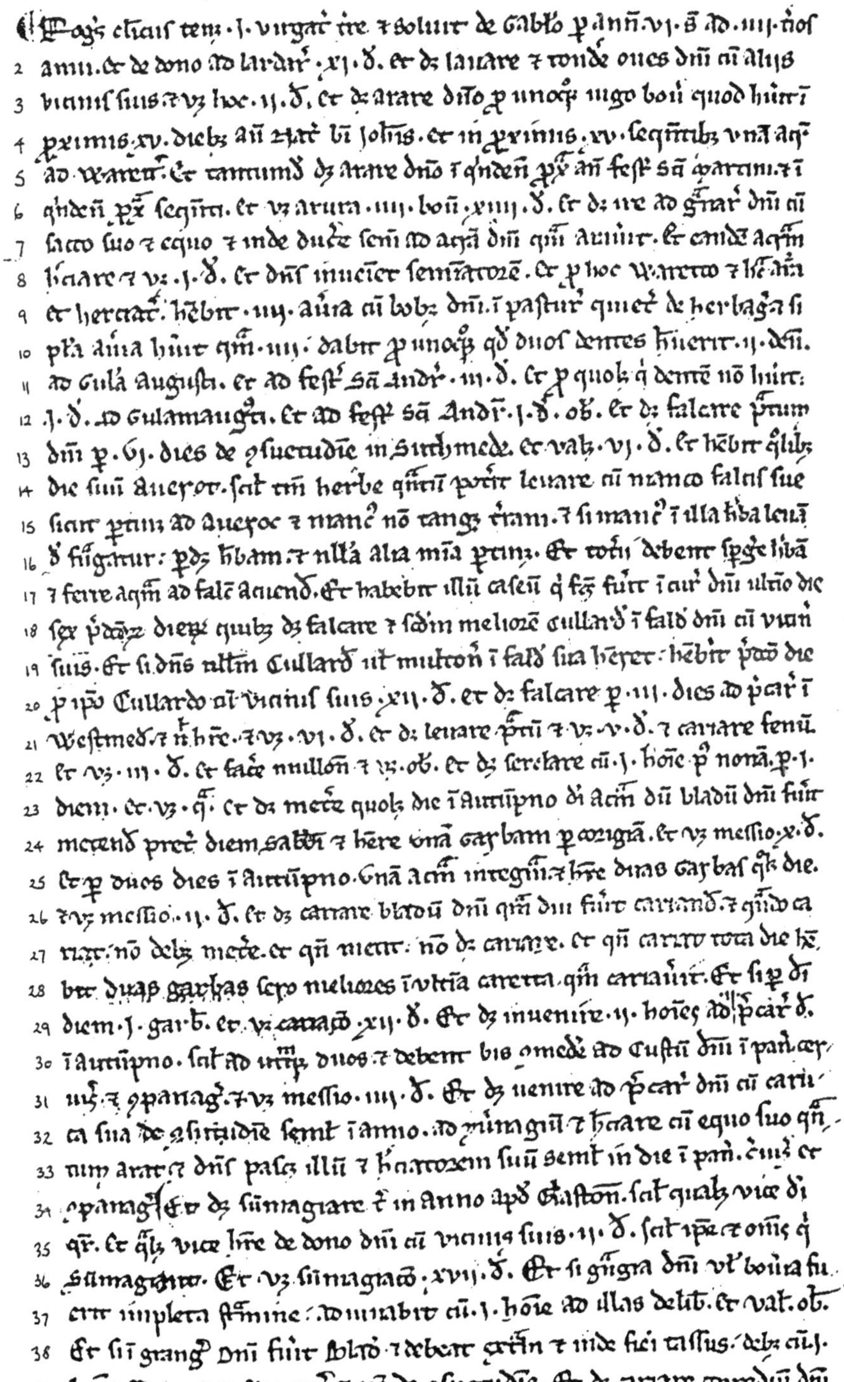

Text VI

It doesn't matter if some of these are hard to read despite being manifestly complete. The important thing is to gain straightaway a confidence that there are after all, so many whole words to work with. The beginner may be already asking, "But how do I know they are whole words?" By the same means as we do to-day, namely, the lack of any marks suggesting abbreviation, in a sequence of letters between two spaces! That puts it at the lowest. With luck, the learner will actually recognise some of them. In my example few will fail to recognise some instances of et, some occurrences of de, arare and quod in line 3, ire ad in line 6, equo and inde in line 7, and so on. Other words are a little more elusive thanks to the use of letter-forms not quite so close to our own. An example of this text duly ringed appears as Text VII on page 9.

You can now go on to use some of these whole words in two quite different ways. First you will build up an alphabet of this scribal hand by attempting to copy from a collection of whole words. Secondly, by a study of the whole words you will try to discover some of the rules of shortening. The techniques you pick up are those you will need when reading other texts.

Wlls Cags eliciis ten. j. virgat terre et soluit de Gablo p annu .vj. s. ad .iiij. t(er)mi(n)os
anni. Et de dono ad Lardar. xj. d. Et debet lauare et tondere oues d(omi)ni cum aliis
vicinis suis et valet hoc .ij. d. Et debet arare d(omi)no per unam acram in(ter) hyemem (quod) h(ab)it in
p(ro)ximis .xv. dieb(us) an(te) (et) post festum s(an)c(t)i Joh(ann)is. Et in p(ro)ximis .xv. sequentib(us) unam acram
ad Waretu(m). Et tame(n) inueniat debet arare d(omi)no i(n) q(ui)ndena p(ro)x(ima) ante fest(um) s(an)c(t)i Martini et i(n)
q(ui)ndena p(ro)x(ima) sequenti. Et valet arura .iiij. bou(m) .xiiij. d. Et debet ire ad g(ra)nar(ium) d(omi)ni cum
sacco suo et equo et inde ducere semen ad acram d(omi)ni q(ua)m arauit. Et eande(m) acram
herciare et val(et) .j. d. Et d(omi)n(u)s inueniet seminatorem. Et p(ro) hoc Waretto et h(ab)eat a(n)i(m)a(li)a
et herciat. h(ab)ebit .iiij. a(n)i(m)alia cum bob(us) d(omi)ni i(n) pastur(a) quiet(a) de herbag(io) et si
plura a(n)i(m)alia h(ab)uerit q(ua)m .iiij. dabit p(ro) unoq(uo)q(ue) q(uo)d duos dentes h(ab)uerit .ij. den(arios).
ad Gulam Augusti. Et ad fest(um) s(an)c(t)i Andr(ee) .iij. d. Et p(ro) quolib(et) q(ui) dentem no(n) h(ab)uerit
.j. d. ad Gulam Augusti. Et ad fest(um) s(an)c(t)i Andr(ee) .j. d. ob. Et debet falcare p(ra)tum
d(omi)ni p(er) .vj. dies de (con)suetudine in Sitthmede. Et val(et) .vj. d. Et h(ab)ebit q(ua)lib(et)
die sum(m)am Aueror. scilicet tantu(m) herbe q(uan)tu(m) poterit leuare cum manico falcis sue
sicut p(er)tinet ad aueror(em) et manic(us) no(n) tangat t(er)ram. Et si manic(us) i(n) illa h(er)ba leuan(da)
d(e)frangatur: p(er)dat h(er)bam et nullam aliam min(us) p(er)tinet. Et toti debent sp(er)g(er)e h(er)bam
i(n) ferre aq(ua)m ad falc(em) acuend(am). Et habebit illu(m) caseu(m) q(ui) f(a)c(tu)s fuit i(n) cur(ia) d(omi)ni ultimo die
sex p(re)d(i)c(t)or(um) dier(um) quib(us) debet falcare et sedem meliore(m) Cullard(um) i(n) fald(a) d(omi)ni cum vicin(is)
suis. Et si d(omi)n(u)s alt(eru)m Cullard(um) n(on) multon(em) i(n) fald(a) sua h(ab)eret: h(ab)ebit p(re)d(i)c(t)o die
p(ro) ip(s)o Cullardo cum vicinis suis .xij. d. Et debet falcare p(er) .iij. dies ad p(re)car(iam) i(n)
Westmed. et n(on) h(ab)ere. et val(et) .vj. d. Et debet leuare p(ra)tum et val(et) .v. d. et cariare fenu(m).
Et val(et) .iij. d. Et facere multon(em) et val(et) ob. Et debet sarclare cum .j. hom(in)e p(ost) nona(m) p(er) .j.
diem et val(et) q(uadrantem). Et debet metere quolib(et) die i(n) autu(m)pno di(midiam) acram du(m) bladu(m) d(omi)ni fuit
metend(um) p(re)t(er) diem sabb(at)i et h(ab)ere una(m) garbam p(ro) corigia(m). Et val(et) messio .x. d.
Et p(er) duos dies i(n) autu(m)pno una(m) acram integ(ra)m et h(ab)ere duas garbas q(ua)lib(et) die
et val(et) messio .ij. d. Et debet cariare bladu(m) d(omi)ni q(ua)m diu fuit cariand(um). et q(ua)n(do) ca
riat: no(n) debet metere. Et q(uan)diu metit: no(n) debet cariare. Et q(ua)n(do) cariat tota die: h(ab)e
bit duas garbas de(?) meliores i(n) ult(im)a careta q(ua)m cariauit. Et si p(er) di(midiam)
diem .j. garb(am). Et val(et) cariagiu(m) .xij. d. Et debet inuenire .ij. hom(in)es ad p(re)car(iam) d(omi)ni
i(n) autu(m)pno. scilicet ad min(us) duos. et debent bis comedere ad custu(m) d(omi)ni i(n) pane cer(uisia)
(con)q(ue)ra et (com)panag(io). et val(et) messio .iiij. d. Et debet uenire ad p(re)car(iam) d(omi)ni cum caru
ca sua de (con)suetudine semel i(n) anno ad minagiu(m) et herciare cum equo suo q(ua)n(do)
(ne)c(essar)i(o) arat. et d(omi)n(u)s pascet illu(m) et herciatorem suu(m) semel in die i(n) pan(e) c(er)uis(ia) et
(com)panag(io). Et debet summagiare semel in anno ap(u)d Glaston. scilicet qualib(et) vice di
q(ua)r(ter). Et q(ua)lib(et) vice h(ab)ere de dono d(omi)ni cum vicinis suis .ij. d. scilicet ip(s)e et om(n)es q(ui)
summagiant. Et val(et) summagiu(m) .xvij. d. Et si g(ra)ngia d(omi)ni vel bou(er)ia fu
erit impleta f(ru)m(en)to: ieminabit cum .j. hom(in)e ad illas del(i)b(erandas). Et val(et) ob.
Et si i(n) grang(ia) d(omi)ni fuit fol(iatu)m(?) debent c(ur)ru(m) et inde fieri tassus debet cum .j.

Building Up An Alphabet

The principle of the reader as writer is well known in education. I myself have found that the attempt to write in a particular hand makes me much more aware of the crucial fine details and, equally, of the general feel or manner of a hand. You are now asked to acquire familiarity with the hand of Text VI - in stages, through the exercises provided. They employ words collected from those ringed in Text VII.

(a) Copying from the source

Make a photocopy of Text **VIII**, and on it have a go at writing exact copies of the words. It is not vital to get every detail right first time (I would say it is impossible!), but for the exercise to bear fruit you need to strive towards accuracy.

As you struggle, you will find yourself asking questions about the way the scribes made the letters, questions like these:

How can I make the little middle line in **e** without it filling in to make a blob?

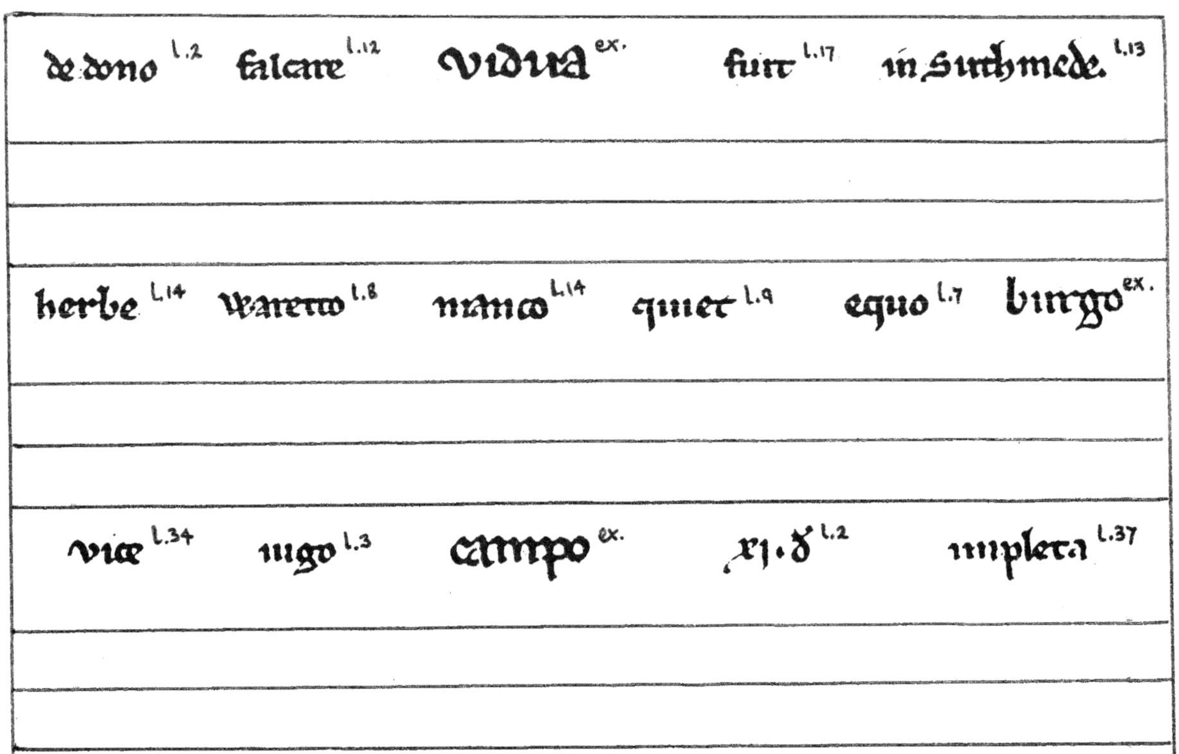

Text VIII

Do the letters touch by accident or are they in some sense joined?

-and more fundamentally-

How many strokes compose the letter? (With experience you will find some hands employ several strokes in a single letter.) 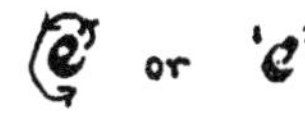

Are the main strokes vertical or diagonal, or curved? 

Is there any reason to think the hand makes vertical strokes in an upwards direction (which is in fact awkward), or is the stroke essentially downwards? 

Am I right in thinking that the scribe regularly makes the pen slide up to begin a downward stroke (making a little hook at the top) and does he end the downward stroke with a hook likewise? These tiny additions or 'serifs' will be important later. 

Does he make his horizontal strokes (few as they are) from left to right or from right to left? (Again you will discover that it is not good for the nib to go from right to left, - unless you use a felt tip.) 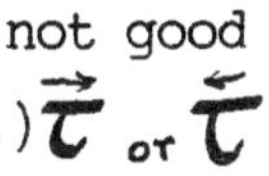

Which is the easier direction for the pen in making diagonals? 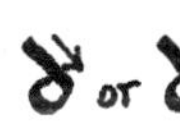
Look also at examples of **v**, **w**, **x** and **y**.

Where exactly is the point at which the scribe begins each letter (and indeed each stroke within the letter) judging by the evidence of the points just raised about easy movement of the pen on the writing-material? 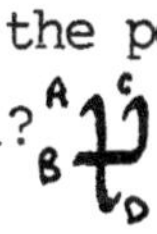

Some letters appear to rise above the top-of-letters line, quite apart from 'ascenders' as in **b**, **d**, **h**, **k**, **l** etc. Which precisely are the letters that regularly do this?[1] Or is this just whim or carelessness?

---

1. The conspicuous example in my text is the letter **a**, but both forms of **s** are capable of this elevation too (look at vicinis suis on line 20 of my ringed text, page 9) . So are consonant **v** and **w**.

Remember, you are not entering a handwriting contest. The object is to get the feel of the scribal hand. As you will discover later, not everything is as clear-cut as the chosen sample suggests - and even has its difficulties anyway! Ambiguous cases will be easier to tackle if you have the sort of practical knowledge that this exercise will give.

At this point it does not matter desperately what the actual letters are nor what Latin words you have here, though it is likely that most students will turn to their Latham (or other dictionary of medieval Latin) for help in identifying strange words. The object of this exercise is to obtain practice in careful copying of the hand of our scribe. So, have a go - writing more than one copy of each word until or unless you feel you cannot do better.

By the end of this small sheet of words (Text VIII) you will have met samples of all the letters in regular use in this hand. In Text IX you will find words that include another **g**, another **a**, another **m**, an extended **i**, two new forms of **r**, **v** used as vowel-**u**, and **u** used as consonant-**v**. If you feel it sufficient, confine your copying to the new forms, reproducing just those letters. The whole words are provided as a context within which to identify each of the new forms.

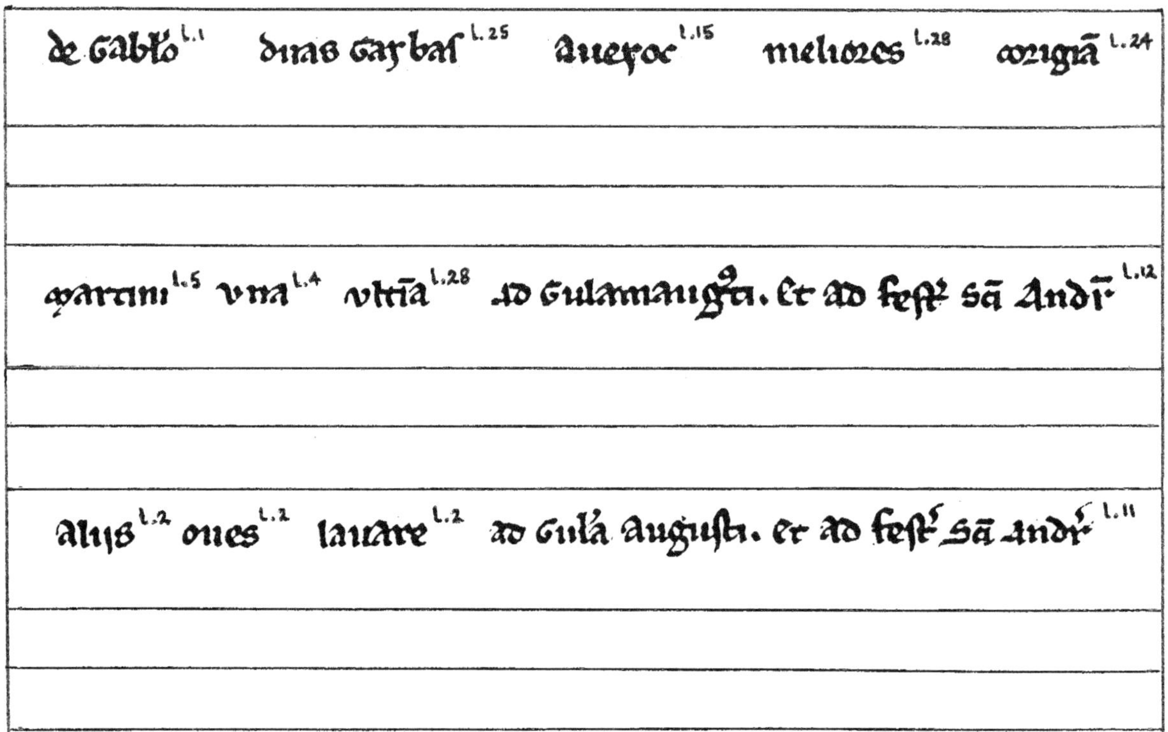

Text IX

(b) Writing out the alphabet

Use a photocopy of Text X to record, letter by letter, what seems to you to be the standard shape of each letter, and also the alternative forms that you have met.

The human hand is not a machine and you will find small differences in the way the scribe writes even the simplest letter. You have to decide on a shape that seems to you to represent the samples best, to sum up most helpfully the average shape of the letter. For example, the head of the letter **a** in my examples varies in length and direction quite considerably. Similarly, the long stroke in **d** has various manifestations. You must decide what is the most typical for the purposes of your alphabet, unless you prefer to record all possible slight differences.

If you feel that one letter could be mistaken for another, note this, and indicate any possible means of distinguishing them. The classic difficulties arise over **c** and **t**, **s** and **f**. Are they a problem in our hand? What about **a** and **d** ? If one letter or another foxes you, leave it for the time being. Sooner or later you will meet it again, in a context where its modern equivalent will not be in doubt.

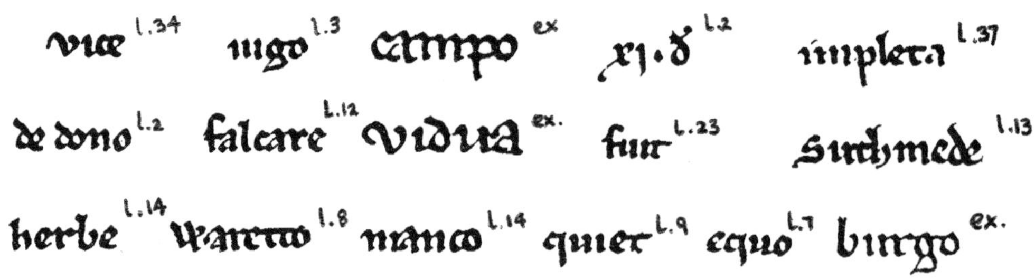

a ______	(i* ______	r ______
______	(______	______
b ______	(j* ______	s ______
______	(______	______
c ______	k ______	t ______
______	______	______
d ______	l ______	(u* ______
______	______	(______
e ______	m ______	(v* ______
______	______	(______
f ______	n ______	w ______
______	______	______
g ______	o ______	x ______
______	______	______
h ______	p ______	y ______
______	______	______
	q ______	z ______
	______	______

* **i/j** - distinct letter forms but with shared sound values. Likewise **u** / **v.**

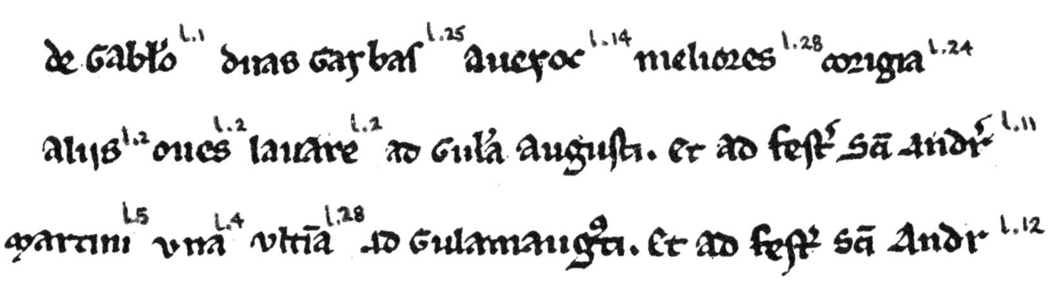

Text X

(c) Practising your alphabet

I offer you now a list of words to write in your scribal hand. Naturally, you have freedom to ignore this opportunity. But I am confident that you will find the attempt both enjoyable and profitable. Make several attempts on each, if necessary. In cases where the scribe has alternative forms of the letter (**s** etc), try both or all.

alia anno dabit debeat dente die filiam hoc illas inde ire licencia metit multo peciam quod tantum tondent acra caretta sicut reddere tassus valoris vendere ferre invenire levare maritare serclare aravit

(d) Correcting your attempt

In Text XI on page 16 you will find how our scribe actually did write those words. In many instances[1] an alternative letter-form could have been used, and you may have opted for such a form. The permutations are numerous, so I have not offered in Text XI alternatives to what the scribe actually wrote.

(e) Further Practice

Text XI is printed with wide spacing so that - if you wish - you can have additional practice in imitating the scribe, preferably on a copy of Text XI.

1. I have marked these with an asterisk.

arga alta anno caretta dabit debeat dente

die ferre filiam fossabit hoc illas inde ire

invenire levare licentia maritare metit multo

peccatum quod reddere secretare sicut tantum

tassus condemto Galoris vendere vidua

Text XI

Some Rules Of Shortening

(a) Preparing a working-base

On page 6 I said that the second use of whole words would be to try, by studying them, to discover some of the rules of shortening. This process is really detective work, exciting and rewarding. And again the techniques you pick up will have much wider application. But before starting, it is necessary to transform your text to something manageable. To allow for the piecemeal gains you will make, you will need a chunk of text widely spaced, as on the next page (Text XII). It was made by cutting between the lines of a copy and pasting the resultant strips (wavy edges and all) on to a clean piece of paper. Photocopy this newly spaced version (Text XII); it will be your working-base for some time.

(b) Recording the whole words

The first practical step I asked of you (page 5) was to locate all the whole words you could, and to mark them with a ring, as on Text VII. Now you need to write out in your own handwriting, on your copy of Text XII, all the whole words that you can spot in those thirteen lines. It is up to you whether you make use of the search you did to produce a ringed text like my Text VII, or whether you use my selection, or whether you make a fresh search in the widely spaced lines of text XII. Do not normalize the spelling at this stage, e.g. by putting **v** for consonant-**u**. Look at Text XIII for guidance as to spacing, but obviously it is best if you refrain from copying my efforts. The idea is for you to have a go yourself.

(c) Numerals

As they usually present little difficulty, you may like next to write in any numerals you can find. Follow the custom demonstrated near the end of line 1 of my text, whereby the last of a series of **i**-s is given a tail, usually transcribed as **j**. On that line you may also spot (what I have left untranscribed) a **j**[=1] and a **vj**[=6].

Rog's cl'icus ten' .j. virgat' t're 7 soluit de gablo p' ann' .vj. s' ad .iiij. t'mi'os
anni. Et de dono ad lardar' .xj. d. Et d3 lauare 7 tond'e oues dni cu' aliis
vicinis suis. 7 val3 hoc .ij. d. Et d3 arare dno p' unoq'q' iugo bou' quod h't' i'
p'ximis .xv. dieb3 an' natal' b'i Joh'is. Et in p'ximis .xv. seq'ntib3 vna ac'
ad warett'. Et tantund' d3 arare dno i' q'nden' p'x' an' fest' sc'i Martini. 7 i'
q'nden' p'x' seq'nti. Et val3 arura .iiij. bou' .xiiij. d. Et d3 ire ad g'nar' dni cu'
sacco suo 7 equo 7 inde duc're sem' ad acr' dni q'm arauit. Et eand' ac'm
h'ciare 7 val3 .j. d. Et dns inueniet seminatore'. Et p' hoc warretto 7 h'ciat'a
et herciat'. h'ebit .iiij. au'ra cu' bob3 dni. 7 i' pastur' quiet' de herbag'. 7 si
p'l'a au'ia h'uit q'm .iiij. dabit p' unoq'q' q'd duos dentes h'uerit .ij. d'n.
ad Gula' Augusti. Et ad fest' sc'i Andr' .iij. d. Et p' quol3 q'd dente' no' h'uit.
.j. d. ad Gulamaugusti. Et ad fest' sc'i Andr' .j. d. ob. Et d3 falcare p'tum
dni p' .vj. dies de co'suetudi'e in Suthmede. Et val3 .vj. d. Et h'ebit q'lib3

Rogs clicus ten3 .j. virgat tre 7 soluit de Gablo p ann .vj. s ad .iiij. tios.
soluit de ad iiij

anni. Et de dono ad lardar. .xj. d. Et de lauare 7 tonde oues dni cu aliis
et de dono ad xj d. et lauare oues aliis

vicinis suis 7 vz hoc .ij. d. Et de arare dno p unoq iugo boū quod habet i
hoc ij d. et arare iugo quod

pximis .xv. dieb3 an estat bi Johis. Et in pximis .xv. sequentib3 vna acr
xv et in xv

ad Waret. Et tantumd de arare dno i quinden px an fest sci Martini 7 i
ad arare martini

quinden px sequent. Et vz arura .iiij. bou .xiiij. d. Et de ire ad granar dni cu
et arura iiij xiiij d. et ire ad

sacco suo 7 equo 7 inde duce semi ad agru dni qn aruint. Et inde acrm
inde ad et

hcare 7 vz .j. d. Et dns inueniet seminatore. Et p hoc Waretto 7 hcan
j d. et et hoc waretto

et hercat. habebit .iiij. aiā cu bob3 dni. i pastur quiet de herbag 7 si
et iiij de

plā aiā habet qm .iiij. dabit p unoqq qd duos dentes habuerit .ij. den.
iiij dabit duos dentes ij den.

ad Gulā augusti. et ad fest sci Andr .iij. d. Et p quolz q dente nō habet
ad augusti et ad iij d. et

.j. d. ad Gulam augti. Et ad fest sci Andr .j. d. ob. Et de falcare prum
j d. et ad j d. et falcare

dni p .vj. dies de csuetudie in Suthmede. Et vab3 .vj. d. Et habebit cib3
vj dies de in Suthmede et vj d. et

(d) <u>Selecting clue-words and preparing them for work</u>

This is the most important stage in your efforts to master this scribe's hand and the conventions he observes. So take your time.

As you read through Text XII looking for whole words to insert in your 'spaced' text, you should find that some of the whole words are linked in obvious ways to adjacent shortened-words. These links provide clues to the full or 'expanded' word. It is important to write down your reasoning at this stage, in case you are puzzled later or need to make use of it.

It pays, therefore, to make a collection of such promising clusters of whole-words and shortened-words, arranged so as to make room for a brief explanation. Text XIVa shows a possible lay-out, and provides the data-base for a preliminary analysis. The important thing is to isolate the words to be studied from the distracting context of other words. Once again it is simply a matter of scissors and paste, using yet another photocopy of the text! The mechanics of this operation may seem tedious, but this business is too important to rush.

Look at each extract on Text XIVa in turn. Can you see any way in which a whole word sheds light on the adjacent part-word? (Incidentally, do not be put off by the fact that in half of the extracts the whole-word is shorter than the part-word next to it.)

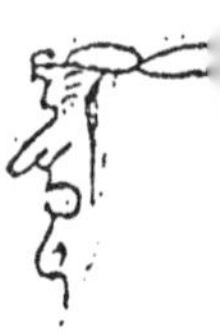

When you have studied the extracts and written your ideas about possible links between whole-word and part-word, turn to Text XIVb, where I have set down briefly the kind of light that can be shed, - some possible links.

line

1. 

2. 

2. 

2. 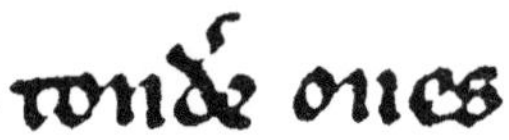

2. 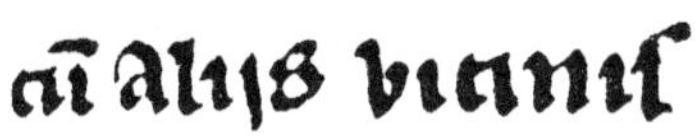

3.
5. 

5. 

6. 

6. 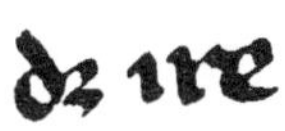

6. 

7. 

8. 

9. 

11.
12. 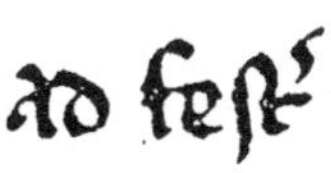

12 

13 

Text XIVa

line

1.  de + ablative (-o). Look up the noun. We find gabulum. So here it is de gabulo.

2.  ad + accusative. Look up the noun. Two forms (m. or f.) Here it could be ad lardarium or ad lardariam.

2. 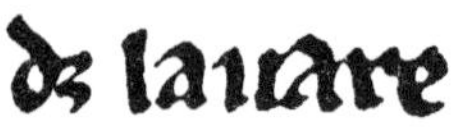 u for v? lavare the infinitive of lavo. Possibly preceded by a verb like possum or volo?

2.  oues for oves (sheep)? tond' = part of tondeo (cut)? (Something to do with shearing sheep?)

2. 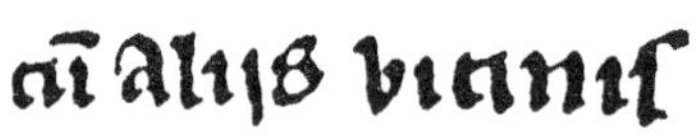 cu' + abl. or dat.pl.[-is] has to be cum + ablative. (with other neighbours?).

3.)
5.)  The same two letters as preceded lavare above, and arare is another infinitive.

5.  First word ends in -i. Could be an adjective agreeing with martini?

6.  vʒ(?) reminds me of dz(?), but there is no following infinitive. Look up arura. (plough-service).

6. 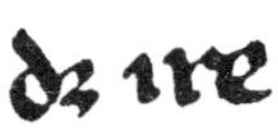 dʒ again, and ire the infinitive of eo (to go).

6. 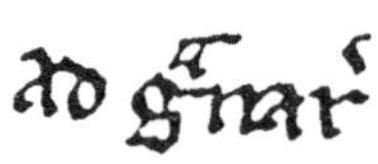 Another ad + accusative. The other word is too difficult to handle at this stage.

7.  Yet another ad. Has to be ad acram or ad acras. (Question: Shall we learn which, s. or pl.?)

9.  de + ablative. Look up herbag-. None of the meanings seems likely to have a plural. So de herbagio.

11. 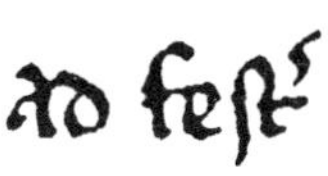 ad again. Look up fest-. Hence ad festum.

12.  Another dʒ + infinitive.

13.  If p is a short word, it could be a preposition. per + accusative perhaps? dies cd.be acc.pl.

Several general points emerge from this study:

(1)  appears to stand for a verb on which the infinitive of some other verb depends.

(2) Prepositions are often written in full, and usually fix the case-ending of a following noun.

(3) Nouns are often unfamiliar to a novice, but reference to a dictionary provides both declension and gender.

(4) While the case of a shortened noun may be thus deducible, it may be harder to discover whether it is singular or plural.

The most striking discovery, embracing all these points, is that some fairly elementary grammatical knowledge yields a good deal of fruit.

Our deductions have so far focused on the words[1] that have been shortened in the text. What of the various marks that are attached by the scribe to these shortened words?

 is unmarked, but what is this z-like element? Surely not the last letter of the alphabet? As for the marks, let us list their occurrences:

‾ occurs in noun, preposition and adjective - 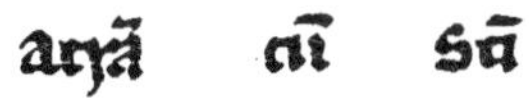

ʻ occurs mostly in nouns - 

Such an array seems to tell us little, but then we have only a tiny piece of text and a handful of examples. More are needed. To produce these I have gone beyond our prepared text (Text XII), comprising only thirteen lines, right back to the full text (Text VII). From this I have taken a longer selection of whole words, together with the shortened words adjacent to them. Study this array in the light of Text XIVb, and then follow closely the analysis that ensues.

---

1. Since our conclusions are bound to be provisional, it is wise to postpone adding our suggested gabulo etc to Text XIII until more detective work has brought confirmation.

line

2 ad lardar'

2 de lauare

2 tondē oues

3 uz hoc .ij. d.

3) 5) de arare

5 sc̄i martini

6 uz arura

6 de ire

7 ad arã

8 uz .j. d.

8 p hoc warecto

9 cũ bobz

12 falcare p'tum

13 p .vij. dies

13 et valz .vj. d.

14 potēt leuare

14 cũ ntanco falcis sue

16 debent sp'ge

17 facere agm̄

17 habebit illũ caseũ

20 de falcare p .iij. dies

20 p ipō Cullardo cũ uianis sui

21 et de leuare p'tũ

21 uz .v. d.

22 et de serclare

22-3 p .j. diem

23 de metē

24 pret' diem

24 vnã garbam

25 p duos dies

26 uz messio .ij. d. et de cariar

29 de inuenire

31 uz messio .iiij. d.

32 cũ equo suo

34 qualz vice

37 impleta t'mine

38 debeat grt'n

Text XVa

line

2  Dealt with in Text XIVb: ad lardariam or ad lardarium

2  See Text XIVb: dz(?) is some verb like possum or volo

2  See Text XIVb: to do with sheep-shearing?

3  For vz se Text XIVb. hoc seems clear, as does ij d

3)
5)  See Text XIVb

5  See Text XIVb

6  See Text XIVb

6 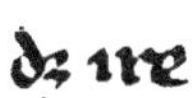 See Text XIVb

7  See Text XIVb

8 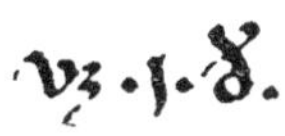 vz again, this time followed by j d..

8  Has to be ablative. Is the  a preposition? pro?

9  If cū = cum, bobz must be ablative. ?bobus from bos, bovis

12  falcare(to mow), but many words have the form p...tum

13  See Text XIVb

13 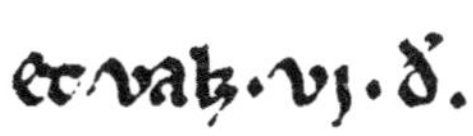 Here valz, followed (like vz) by a sum of money.

14  levare (infinitive) suggests part of possum for pot-

14  cū' for cum again. sue? = classical suae?

16  debent + infinitive?  looks like per-. Hence sperg..e?

17  ferre and a...m (accusative?) acram? aquam?
You can carry water, but not acres!

TEXT XVB

17  habebit + direct object? If so illum caseum? Therefore -ū = -um?

20 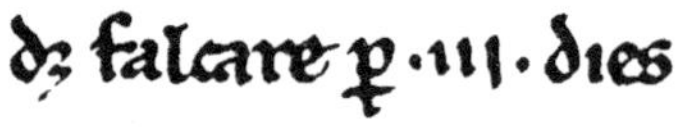 dz + infinitive. per iij dies?

20  pro and cum again?

21  Looks like line 12  . -ū- again = -um? p...tum = ?

21  vz v d.

22  Look up the infinitive. serclare = to hoe or weed.

22-3 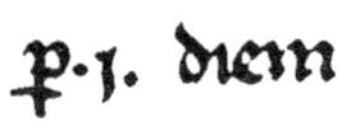 per j diem seems to make sense.

23  dz usually + inf. So metare / metere / metire ?

24 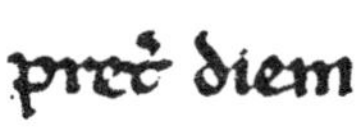 Could be preposition preter + accusative.

24 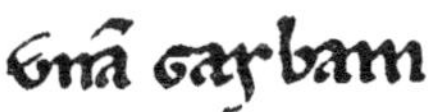 Surely unam garbam? So again -ā- = -am?

25  per again.

26  Both vz and dz.

29  dz, and is it invenire?

31  vz messio again, but this time 4d.

32  This must be cum equo suo.

34  Presumably **q** and not **g** at the beginning.

37 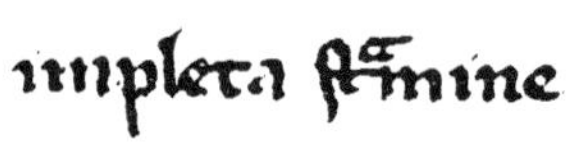 impleta. Second word begins with **f** or **s**? It ends with -mine. Few clues so far on -t-.

38 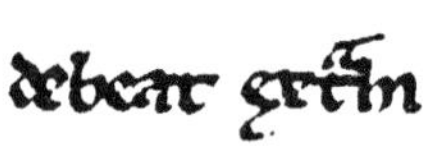 debeat. The 2nd word begins with ex-; then -t- again; it ends with -m / -ln / -hi?

TEXT XVc

Some deductions from Text XVa

It will be useful at this point if I think aloud through some of the examples that appear in Text XVa, to make visible the thinking involved in decipherment. You will probably soon be content to make the kind of abbreviated notes that I made in Text XIVb. It is important to notice that there is no virtue in taking items in the order of the text; go for items that can be grouped because they have some common element.

Glancing through the fuller collection of whole-words we are drawn to the verb infinitives preceded by  . Surely we can crack this one?

1.2		(to wash)	1.21		(to make[hay])
1.3		(to plough)	1.22	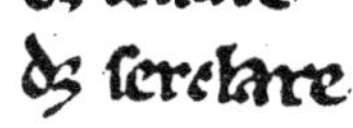	(to weed)
1.6	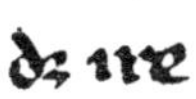	(to go)	1.26	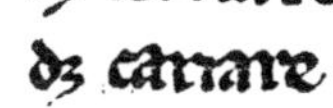	(to cart)
1.12	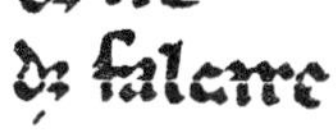	(to mow)	1.29	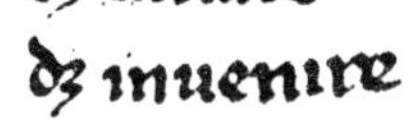	(to find)
			1.31	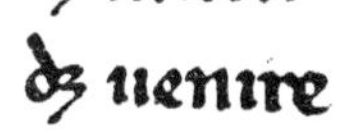	(to come)

There is nothing here resembling the Accusative and Infinitive construction so beloved of school text-books: no verb of saying, no obvious accusative. So we pursue the possibility already raised that these infinitives are dependent on other verbs, such as possum or volo. Could  represent such a verb?

Fortunately our memories are jogged by the occurrence, not far from the infinitives of some verbs, of debent written in full (lines 16 and 30). Further search reveals on line 27 the in-between form  .

This all seems very plausible, but it leaves unresolved the precise significance of the  at the end of  and  . It could represent any of the various endings of the verb debeo. True, apart from debent the only verbs written in full in our sample seem to be third person singular: solvit line 1; dabit line 10; habebit line 17; arat line 33; debeat line 38. Consulting our "material...similar in kind"[1] in Text IV, page 4, we see that debet is in fact very common.

---

1. See the advice given on page 3.

So, provisionally, we interpret  and  as debet, with the corollary that  could regularly stand for -et[1].

That page embodied a particular conclusion and a procedure, seemingly lengthy. It must be borne in mind that what takes some time to write out is but the work of a few moments to think out. Furthermore, the kind of operation in which we are now engaged is one that will be necessary later on when you move on to tackle more difficult hands.

Our hypothesis needs testing. We must examine the various other occurrences of  . Scanning the source text we find these:

1.1 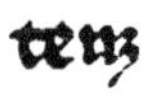 1.4  1.15  1.33 

1.4  1.9  1.18 

Some of these are perplexing, but some have recognisable elements: 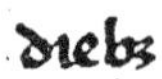 must surely be diebus,  bobus, and  be quibus So in these cases at least,  cannot represent -et.

However, others, equally identifiable, are clearly verbs:
 tenet,  tanget,  pascet

We have so far ignored another big group of  items, the numerous occurrences of . In most cases it is followed by a sum of money (anything from a halfpenny [ob. = obolus] to 17d). Very conveniently once again we have an in-between form, on line 13,  . This points us to valet as the full form, an interpretation confirmed again by reference to our Text IV (page 4).

You are reminded at this point that such a mass of clues could be investigated in a variety of ways. Ours is simply one model. The model has several key components:

(i) assembling a set of similar instances. (Working from a single word or phrase is less fruitful.)

---

1. To avoid misleading you, I should add here that while the -et value of 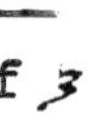 is pretty well universal, this double abbreviation,  = d[eb][et], is local.

(ii) inspecting the known and the unknown elements to see in what ways they can be linked, grammatically speaking.

(iii) looking for evidence elsewhere that might clarify or clinch the enquiry.

(iv) carefully wording a general rule.

(v) testing the rule against as-yet-unused examples.

The procedure will, I believe, form the basis of future good practice. Its upshot in this case is a slightly complicated rule which I shall fully formalise a little later on. I shall also suggest putting it into practice. But first we shall look at another very distinctive sign that appeared as we scrutinised our collection of whole words with their neighbours.

Scattered in our collection are the following, made distinctive by the presence of the raised or 'superscript' sign  , somewhat resembling modern handwritten lower case **a**, or a **u** with a line along its top[1]:

 (line 17) and  (line 12)

The first is unmistakably ferre a**qua**m, in which case the sign could stand for -ua-. The other is a little less obvious, until one recalls that falcare means "to mow" and that the term for what-one-mows is "meadow" (**pra**tum). In this case the little sign stands for -ra-.

Once more we try to test these possibilities. Again some instances present a little difficulty, but both these possibilities seem to be confirmed. Unmistakable are words beginning with **q**- :

 (quam lines 7,10,26,28)  (quantum lines 32-3) 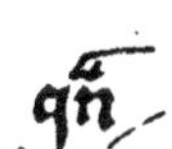

- with the reasonable possibility that after **q** the sign means -**ua**-.

Equally persuasive are the following:

 (integram line 25) with the preceding (acram), yielding

1. In some hands the sign is just an open (raised) **u**, with no line over it.

the not improbable expression "a whole acre", as well as

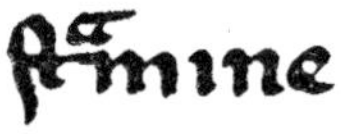 (stramine line 37) which, with the preceding impleta, yields "filled with straw". Encouraged by these, we more boldly read

(line 16) 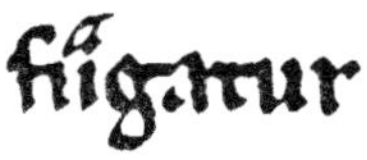 as frangatur and 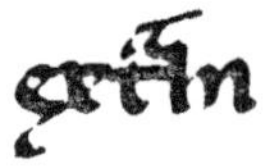 (line 38) as extrahi.

Accuracy requires us to note the instances which do NOT fit. The sign  must indicate simply -a- in at least these cases:

if  (1.7) stands for acram, and if  (1.8) stands for hac, as is suggested by the nearby hoc. At later points in the book I shall deal with  (lines 5 and 6) and 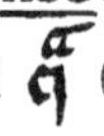 (1.23).

It is time to consolidate the gains we have made in our search for signs of shortening. Following our previous attempts to write words with our scribe's alphabet, it is sensible to put these signs of shortening into practice. Try to write these words in our scribe's hand, putting  or  wherever you think they could possibly have been used:

quarta grangia metet quando cadet[1]

Next you need to make sure you have a clear view of the points we have been discussing. I suggest that you make notes summarising the uses of the signs  and , insofar as we have been able to form tentative ideas about them. As in any study, the effort to organise your understanding by making notes will itself help to make the gains more secure. On the next page you will find a summary that includes points made in two separate places: in the course of the full discussion on pages 27-30, and in the more abbreviated comments contained on Texts XVb and XVc (pages 25 and 26). If you have not yet done so, you should now examine Texts XVb and XVc carefully. Please remember, however, that the organisation of my summary was not given on tablets of stone on Mt Sinai, and you may prefer some other way of arranging the points.

---

1. See Key (page 118).

SUMMARY OF SIGNS USED IN SHORTENED WORDS

(a) Signs **on** the line of print that look like letters

but are, perhaps, just signs:

ꝫ at the end of a verb seems to stand for <u>-et</u>.

bꝫ seems to stand for <u>-bus</u>.

In doubly shortened words:

dꝫ seems to signify <u>debet</u>.

vꝫ seems to signify <u>valet</u>.

(b) Signs **above** the line of print.

What looks like a little **u** with a line over it [ᵘ̄]

seems to represent <u>-ra-</u>, or <u>-ua-</u> (after **q**).

A line over a vowel (especially at word-ends)

possibly represents <u>-m</u>.

(c) Signs **below** the line - modifying one particular letter.

A Horizontal line through the descender of **p** [ꝑ]

means <u>-per-</u> (on its own or as a part-word).

An angular mark through (or near) the descender of **p** [ꝓ]

means <u>-pro-</u> (on its own or otherwise).

Note that the tentative tone of this summary reflects the very limited sample of Latin on which it is based.

The Use Of Parallel Expressions

In the samples of text used to build up our scribe's alphabet were two versions of a particular group of words:

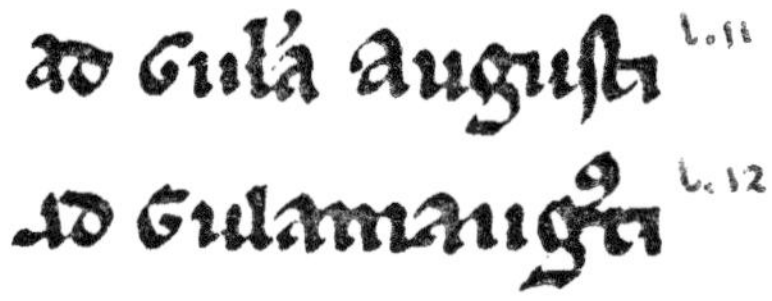

These gave us two forms of the letter **a** (in ad) and a new form (other than the modern form) of the letter **s**. They also introduced a distinctive mark or sign to help the reader make sense of a shortened word.[1] Evidently,

and hence **9** has something to tell us about the lost -us-: it could simply say, "At this point letters have been omitted" (i.e. augti is not a complete word, - of course); it could also imply that the lost letters had been between -g- and -t- , although this is a less reliable inference, as will appear later; no less possible is the simple equation, 9 = -us-. We need further information, more clues. As we shall see in a moment, it is important to observe that the **9** we have been discussing is superscript, i.e. above the text.

Two lines later we find a useful series of items:

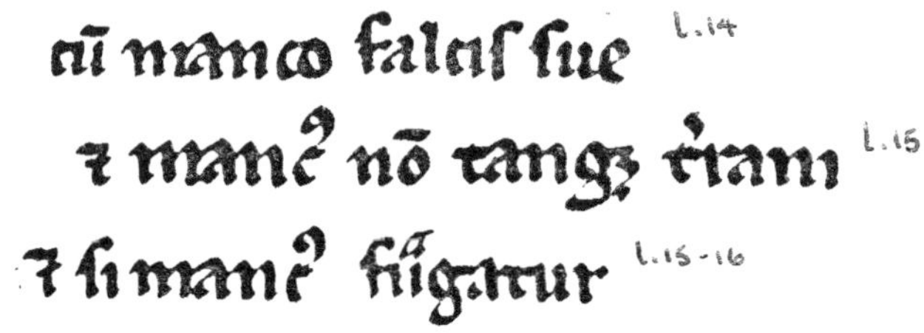

We can ignore all other words and signs and see here strong support for the idea that **9** could mean -us-, yielding here the nominative manc**us** to match the ablative manco.

Alas! The attentive student's eye may have fallen also on some

---

1. I leave on one side at this stage the other parallelism, that between  and 

examples that seem not to fit this view of ꝰ:

line 30 

lines 31, 34 

line 32 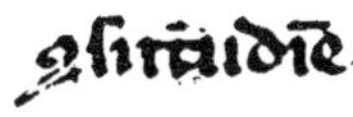

line 39 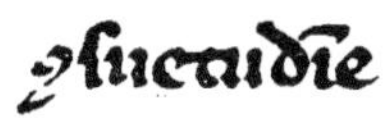

Obviously, -us- is out of the question. So **9** must have at least two distinct meanings or values. Fortunately, careful inspection of this last batch points the way to interpreting one of these two other uses. 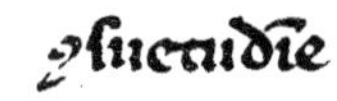 could be consuetudine (minus the last **n**), and 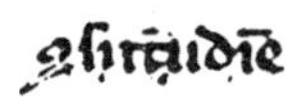 must be the same word misspelt. If so, at the beginning of a word, and NOT superscript, **9** appears to mean **con-**. The other two examples are slightly obscure, thanks to the presence of other signs. We have simply to bear in mind the rule of assimilation (familiar in numerous English derivatives[1]) whereby con- becomes **com-** before **b**, **m**, and **p**. This gives us commed- and companag-, plausible enough part-words. Reference to a dictionary gives us the verb commedo and the noun companagium. The only other **9** on our page (p^{9} - p line 22) is best left in limbo for the time being, since it is manifestly neither con- nor -us.

 EXERCISE. Use **9** to write the following words in our scribe's hand:

unus campus continuos redditus communis Folcredus
unius quietus albus Bercarius predictus constant[ia] [2]

You now have additions to make to your notes on Signs of Shortening. Locate in your existing array of signs the appropriate homes for ꝰ and ꝯ .[3] Indicate the letters they seem to represent.

---

1. cf.co**mb**ine, co**mm**it, and co**mp**are (but co**nd**emn, co**nf**ess, co**ng**regate etc.).
2. For his version, see Key (page 118).
3. I have used the sign **9** for these two distinct signs because their resemblance is often more marked than here. Consult Hector p.32, and Johnson and Jenkinson p.60. (See FURTHER READING.)

Back To The Transcript

It is now time to put our provisional findings to use. We return to our spaced version of part of the model text, already doctored by the insertion of whole words and numbers. (See Text XIII p.19) I suggest that you add any words that can now be deduced on the strength of our findings; for reasons of space and to assist checking, newly transcribed words should be written slightly lower than those already inserted. See Text XVI, p.35, for this suggestion and to see evidence of what seem to be the chief gains from our detective work so far.

Rog's clics tenet .j. virgat' tre & soluit de gablo p ann .vj. d ad .iiij. t'mos 1.

tenet i Soluit de gabulo per vi ad iiij

anni. Et de dono ad lardar' .xj. d. et d3 lauare & tond'e oues dni cu aliis 2.

et de dono ad ↳ lardarium xj d. et debet lauare oues cum aliis

vicinis suis & v3 hoc .ij. d. et d3 arare dno p unoq3 iugo boum quod habet i 3

valet hoc ij d. et debet arare pro iugo quod

pximis .xv. diebz ante natl' bi Johis. et in pximis .xv. sequentibz unam acr' 4

xv diebus et in proximis xv ...tibus unam

ad waretu. Et tantumd' d3 arare dno i qnden pxi ante fest' sci martini & i 5

[Letham has both] ad warectam/um? debet arare prox.... martini

qnden px' sequenti. et v3 arura .iiij. boum .xiiij. d. et d3 ire ad granar' dni cum 6

prox... et valet arura iiij boum xiiij d. et debet ire ad ↳ granar-ium cum

sacco suo & equo & inde duc'e sem ad acra dni qua arauit. et eand' acra 7

suo equo inde ad ↳ acram quam et eandem acram

herciare & v3 .j. d. et dns inueniet seminatore. et p hoc waretto & hac 8

valet j d. et et pro hoc waretto hac

et herciac' habebit .iiij. aiā cum bobz dni i pastur' quiet' de herbagio si 9

et iiij cum bobus de herbagio si

plura aiā habet qm .iiij. dabit p unoq3 qd duos dentes habuerit .ij. den. 10

quam iiij dabit pro duos dentes ij den.

ad Gulam Augusti. et ad fest' sci Andr' .iij. d. et p quolibet q dente no habet 11

ad augusti et ad ↳ festum iij d. et pro dentem

.j. d. ad Gulamaugusti. et ad fest' sci Andr' .j. d. ob. et d3 falcare pratum 12

j d. Gulamaugusti et ad ↳ festum j d. et debet falcare pratum

dni p .vj. dies de consuetudine in Suthmede. et val3 .vj. d. et habebit qlibz 13

per vj dies de consuetudine in Suthmede et valet vj d. et

Text XVI

In the course of this work you may well have noticed certain commonly recurring features of the original manuscript text.

⁊ occurs frequently, appears to stand for a whole word, and at least sometimes occurs between parallel items:

sacco ⁊ equo   lavare ⁊ tondere

It has to be a conjunction, by far the most likely being **et**.

dns, dni, dno. Surely forms of dominus - the lord being the party most concerned with what the tenant owes as duty (debet).

At the end of lines 3 and 5 and in the middle of line 4, an inconspicuous ī may have caught your eye, apparently representing a whole word. The first of them is followed by the words

ꝑximis.xv.diebꝫ

These you are now competent to transcribe as proximis xv diebus - dative or ablative plural. It looks as if ī stands for in (+ the ablative here). This guess is confirmed later in line 4 by this:

in ꝑximis.xv.seq̄ntibꝫ

The last word of this phrase may bother you, but **in** proximis xv is indisputable. We have therefore to modify our provisional rule about a line over a vowel. This new evidence requires a formula offering **-m-** and **-n-** as alternatives for the meaning of the line over **-i-**, at least. Caution restrains us from a wider conclusion.

At this point, therefore, some more detective work seems needed. However, that in itself will be easier if we once again update the

transcript.

(1) Insert (on a third line) et for all instances of ⁊ [1].

(2) Write **in** in full wherever appropriate.

(3) Write in the variants of dominus for dns, dno etc.

---

1. Be prepared for 7, an un-barred version of this sign for et = "and".

By now you may feel confident enough to attempt partial transcriptions of some words. On the first line virgat' is obvious, as is lardar' on line 2. It is sufficient at this point to write parts of words, as I have just done. However, you may recall that on page 22, in Text XIVb, we were tempted by the ad to look up lardar' in Latham, so that we could supply an accusative ending. Do not get bogged down in looking words up if this proves difficult, but by all means complete part-words where the ending seems beyond doubt, i.e. where it is determined by grammatical considerations. Here virgat' seems to be the object of tenet, hence accusative, hence virgatam. I would strongly urge on you the rule, When in doubt, leave it out. It is wiser to leave a partially transcribed word than to make a guess. Later we shall deal more exactly with the completing of unfinished words. Text XVIIa shows the sort of update you might produce. Text XVIIb is a tidied-up version of the same thing.

Having made these new additions to the transcript you may well begin to be impatient. Surely the end is in sight? Can we not proceed to complete the transcription? The answer is No. Making a transcript is not the main purpose of the book, and to pursue that short-term objective exclusively would interfere with the main purpose. Basically, the partial transcript is a record of your gains as you go along. It will serve as a spring-board to further learning, precisely because I have chosen most of the examples from this one text. The more familiar it becomes, the more readily you will grasp the point of the various examples. Of course, making the transcript is also useful practice in transcribing generally, and the piecemeal progress you are making illustrates the nature of transcription when you are inexperienced or when the text is difficult, a stage by stage process.

I have spoken of the advisability of building up a transcription in stages. This arises from the almost vicious circle inherent in text so thoroughly abbreviated. Deductions depend principally on context. But the context of a particular abbreviated word is usually itself made up of other abbreviated words. That is why we began with whole words, and why we still proceed from one new conclusion to another.

Rog... tenet i virgat... et soluit de gabulo per vi ad iiij 1.

et de dono ad ↳ lardarium xj d. et debet lauare et oues domini cum aliis 2.

vicinis suis et valet hoc ij d. et debet arare domino pro uno..... iugo bo.... quod in 3

proximis xv diebus Joh... et in proximis xv ....tibus unam acr.. 4

[Letham has both] ad warect am/ums tantumd... debet arare domino in prox.... fest... martini et in 5

prox... seq...ti et valet arura iiij boum xiiij d. et debet ire ad ↳ granar..ium domini cum 6

et suo et equo et inde du......sem... ad ↳ acram domini quam ara...... et eandem acram 7

h.....iare et valet j d. et dominus inu....et sem......... et pro hoc waretto et hac ar..... 8

et herc..... .....bit iiij cum bobus domini in pastur.. quiet.. de herbagio et si 9

p..a a....a h..it quam iiij dabit pro uno... -q... duos dentes ......erit ij den. 10

ad Gu... augusti et ad ↳ festum Andr... iij d. et pro quo..... dentem non 11

j d. ad Gulamaug...... ....usti et ad ↳ festum Andr... j d. et debet falcare pratum 12

domini per vj dies de consuetudine in suthmede et valet vj d. et 13

Rog's clicus ten' .j. virgat' t're 7 soluit de Gablo p ann' .vj. s' ad .iiij. t'ios

Rog... tenet j virgat.. et soluit de gabulo per vj s. ad iiij

anni. Et de dono ad lardar' .xj. d'. Et d3 lauare 7 tonde' oues dni cu' aliis

et de dono ad lardarium xj d. et debet lauare et oues domini cum aliis

vicinis suis. 7 va3 hoc .ij. d'. Et d3 arare dno p uno q'q3 iugo bou' quod h'uit i'

vicinis suis et valet hoc ij d. et debet arare domino pro uno... iugo bo... quod in

p'ximis .xv. dieb3 an' nat' b'i Joh'is. Et in p'ximis .xv. sequ'tib3 una' acr'

proximis xv diebus Joh... et in proximis xv ....tibus unam acr...

ad Warect'. Et tantumd' d3 arare dno i' q'nden' p'x' an' fest' s'ci martini. 7 i'

ad warectam et tantumd.. debet arare domino in prox... fest... martini in

q'nden' p'x' sequ'ti. Et va3 arura .iiij. bou' .xiiij. d'. Et d3 ire ad g'nar' dni cu'

prox... seq....ti et valet arura iiij boum xiiij d. et debet ire ad granarium domini cum

sacco suo 7 equo 7 inde duc' sem' ad acra' dni qua' arauit. Et eande' acra'

suo et equo et inde du... sem.. ad acram domini quam ara.... et eandem acram

h'ciare 7 va3 .j. d'. Et dns inueniet seminatore'. Et p hoc Waretto 7 h'c ar'a

h....are et valet j d. et dominus inu... et sem....... et pro hoc waretto et hac ar.....

Et herciat' h'ebit .iiij. a'ia cu' bob3 dni i' pastur' quiet' de herbag' 7 si

et herc..... .....bit iiij cum bobus domini in pastur.. quiet.. de herbagio et si

pl'a a'ia h'uit qua' .iiij. dabit p uno q'q3 q'd duos dentes h'uerit .ij. den'.

p.....a a....a h... it quam iiij dabit pro uno.....q.... duos dentes h... erit ij den.

ad Gula' augusti. Et ad fest' s'ci Andr' .iij. d'. Et p quol3 q' dente' no' h'uit

ad Gu... augusti et ad festum Andr... iij d. et pro quo... dentem non

.j. d'. ad Gulamaugusti. Et ad fest' s'ci Andr' .j. d'. ob'. Et d3 falcare p'tum

j d. ad Gulamaugusti, et ad festum Andr... j d. et debet falcare pratum

dni p .vj. dies de co'suetudi'e in Suthmede. Et va3 .vj. d'. Et h'ebit c'lib3

domini p. vj dies de consuetudine in Suthmede et valet vj d. et

Not One-For-One

This chapter is by way of a diversion. We turn away from medieval Latin to modern languages to establish some important principles, uncontroversial, but possibly apt to be taken for granted. Students of medieval Latin texts will, I believe, cope better with certain anomalies if they are aware that similar features occur in modern English and even in French, Dutch, German etc.

Consider these numbers: 1473 8904 4256. It is difficult to imagine any symbolic representation less ambiguous than the numerals in use to-day. Indeed, they are not ambiguous. But imagine a reader unfamiliar with our system, - let's say an ancient Roman. Explain that these replace his cumbrous system of letters; tell him that i = 1, ii = 2, iii = 3 and so on. You would find it rather harder to explain that in our three examples the figure **4** means respectively **400**, **4**, and **4000**. We, of course, have no problem in interpreting the **4**s by virtue of their 'place'. The context makes all clear.

Or consider the humble dot: • How diverse are its meanings! To stay within the realm of mathematics first, it serves as a decimal point and as the sign of a recurring decimal, quite a different thing. Fortunately, the position of the dot makes clear which meaning it has. There is a greater variety of use for the dot in verbal text. It serves to provide an additional clue to the identity of lower-case **i** (a clue, incidentally, not used in our Latin MSS); in a lower position it is a punctuation mark, as the full-stop (which also appears unobtrusively in the sentence-enders **?** and **!**); it is also used in the unofficial punctuation mark beloved of novelists and letter-writers, **.....** (usually to mean, "We leave the rest to your imagination!"); finally it serves to announce an abbreviation, i.e. that a group of letters represents a word of which these letters are some part, as in "etc."

When we turn to written letters, things start to become complicated. Take **c**, for example. I have no doubt you will concede that this visual symbol stands for at least two <u>sounds</u> as in the word '**c**on**c**ede' itself, of course. **s** is even more versatile, serving not only for the soft-**c** sound in **sit**, but for **z** in **has**, and when doubled it can signify **sh** as in percu**ss**ion as well as the emphasized or prolonged soft-**s** as in hi**ss**.

Not only can one letter represent more-than-one sound, but equally one sound can be represented by various letters:

quay **k**ing **c**an **ch**asm o**f** **v**ery

finish **Ph**ilip lei**s**ure **j**e-ne-sais-quoi

It would seem appropriate to mention again here the alternative forms of some letters in our scribal hand:

These may be seen as distinct signs standing for the same thing.

On the fringes of respectable English we are perhaps less surprised to find ambiguity. The colloquial forms of the auxiliary verbs be, have and do are perfectly intelligible, even when written, but it is still the case that "He'**s**" could stand for "He **is**" and "He **has**". We must not lose sight of the fact, however, that in this as in all the instances we have mentioned the context leaves the reader or listener in no doubt. "He's lost" can only mean "He **is** lost" whereas "He's lost his wits" can only mean "He **has** lost his wits".

The principle I hope I have established so far is the very obvious, but important, truth that in language or even in tight symbolic systems like mathematics one sign can have more than one meaning and, inversely, that more than one sign may be available to stand for a particular meaning. The absolutely crucial second principle is that a single sign is not interpreted in a vacuum, but always in context. Its physical position on the page or line may be important; the symbols immediately adjacent to it may act as signals; and finally the larger linguistic context of grammar and meaning limits the possibilities.

There is a further complication, best introduced by a glance at these familiar non-words:

Mr. and **Mrs.** John Brown J.C.Brown **Esq.**

All of these abbreviations illustrate one use of the dot already sketched; they represent words of which the given letters are a part:

Maste**r**[1] **M**ist**r**es**s**[1] **Esq**uire

However, distinctions can be drawn in the way in which the surviving letters are chosen. In the first example (Master), the abbreviated form consists of simply the first and last letters, with the entire middle chunk of the word omitted. In the second (Mistress), two little rows of letters are dropped (-ist- and -es-) but the single letter that separates them is preserved in the final abbreviation. From the third example (Esquire) we simply eliminate the final four letters of the original whole word.

As additional examples of these processes we may offer
Bp. for Bishop Cdr. for Commander Ed. for Editor.

You will be correct if you suppose that I have drawn attention to this particular classification of abbreviations because it is found in medieval Latin texts. It is reasonable to employ the terms omission, contraction and suspension for the three processes of shortening that we have described, though (as elsewhere in matters academic) there is no universally agreed usage, nor indeed an agreed system of classification. We adopt this one here because it works well with the very typical hand that is our model.

Unfortunately, only by cheating a little can I illustrate from modern conventions a feature of medieval writing that perhaps gives novices most trouble. We are familiar in modern practice with the caret (‸) to indicate the omission of material from a text (manuscript or otherwise). If asked to describe this device we would undoubtedly say it looks like an inverted **v**. Thus one might say that this angular shape has two uses:

---

1. It is not relevant here that we nowadays pronounce **Mrs** as "Missus" and **Mr** as "Mister" - and even spell them that way; the shortened forms came into existence before the pronunciation was corrupted.

(i) To indicate the omission of material without also being specific about the amount or content of the omission - this being indicated separately and explicitly, if at all.

(ii) To indicate the sound also heard at the end of the word "of".

As we have admitted, this account coyly passes over the fact that in one of its uses the angular shape is inverted.[1] Nevertheless, sympathetic readers may be willing to go along with the story as a way-in to the difficult notion that a single sign may serve either a specific or a non-specific purpose.

EXERCISES

1. The letter **a** can be found as a single vowel in written or printed English words where all sorts of vowel sounds are actually heard. Make a collection of words that have **a** representing different sounds There are at least eight different sounds to be found.
2. To what extent was there one-for-one correspondence between letter and sound in the Latin you learnt? Which letters could have more than one pronunciation? Which letters shared the same sound?
3. If you examine our model text carefully, you will find at various points the scribe has made a light oblique stroke. These are of no great significance to you as a novice reader. However, it might be useful to identify the various occurrences, copy them together with adjacent letters or words, and arrange them in groups according to their exact position relative to other features (above the line of letters, or ....).
4. This is a good place to prepare the ground for a later chapter. Look up the following English words. You will have no difficulty in discovering their common meaning in English. You may benefit from discovering their various derivations.

erase **expunge** **cancel** **obliterate**

---

1. Even more uses can be identified if we turn to French, which has another inverted **v** in its circumflex accent (^), and if we turn to Mathematics, where **v** laid on its side means "greater than" (>) or "less than" (<).

A Grammatical Chapter

I felt compelled to devote my last chapter to making my point about the variability of uses of signs. I could not allow you to proceed believing that scribal abbreviations are used consistently, nor that such seeming inconsistency was peculiar to them. However, we are not yet ready to make a detailed analysis of the uses of signs of abbreviation; we shall adhere to our practice of building on what we know, or have established. In fact, in this chapter you should disregard obvious differences among the signs of shortening that appear in the examples given, and just accept that they mark the omission of a letter or letters.

In this chapter the 'known' is a set of three very elementary grammatical rules in Latin. Readers whose school Latin is not recent need not blench; the rules really are elementary, and we have already called on them in a matter-of-fact way.

1. PREPOSITIONS. ad acrā we surmised on p.22 must stand for ad acram on the grounds that ad is followed by the accusative case. (It is logically possible that the noun might be plural, acra**s**.) So, where a noun is left incomplete or 'suspended' we can often complete it by reference to a preceding preposition:

 ad custu**m** domini  de herbag**io**

By this stage you have probably noticed that often the preposition is itself abbreviated in some way; we have already met per and pro, and the rule about a line above a vowel indicating an **m** or an **n** enabled us to recognise in and cum. Consequently, we can complete these:

 per annum  in pastura 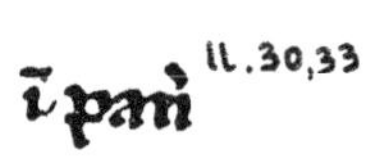 in pane 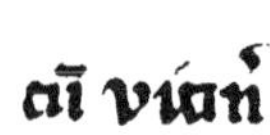 cum vicin**is** 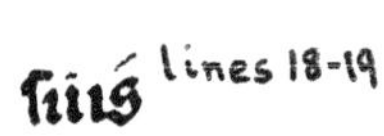 /[1]suis

2. CONCORD (or AGREEMENT) - illustrated in our last example. This rule is familiar to students of European languages. It requires any word that qualifies a noun to agree with it in all relevant respects[2]. In modern

---

1. suis is cut off from cum vicinis in the text by the ending of line 18.
2. It also requires agreement between a verb and its grammatical subject.

languages this means in Gender and Number (and occasionally in Case):

une fille der mannen 't kind el nino las cartas

Latin, of course, does include case. Hence we find on lines 6-7 of our text, cum sacco suo, suo agreeing with sacco in case, number and gender, - ablative singular masculine. In the example just quoted after a preposition, we had, in fact, not one but two clues to the completion of the abbreviated word vicin': not only was there the cum preceding it, but the suis following it. In this instance we could have deduced vicinis from suis without the help of the cum. This element of redundancy in language is more prevalent than is commonly realised, and the novice reader of medieval texts should be grateful for it. It appears again in the second of these examples:

 l.24 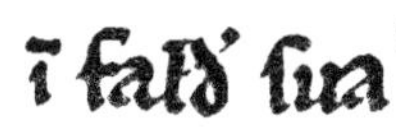 l.19

unam garbam in falda sua

3. SUBJECT - VERB - OBJECT. To keep the examples reasonably clear I have limited them here to expressions that do not introduce new kinds of abbreviation. But I have quietly introduced our third category of grammatical clues. I removed unā garbam from its context; the preceding word (if we write it in full) was habere, and this verb clearly has unam garbam as its direct object. The use of the cases in Latin without a preposition is seldom obscure in medieval texts, and readers soon become oblivious to the endings of nominatives and accusatives; whether they are shortened or written in full scarcely enters the consciousness of a reader who has grasped the presence of the relationships of subject or object of some verb. We have previously glanced (page 26) at one instance:

habebit illū caseū has to be habebit illum caseum

- for the grammatical reason that "will have" clearly has "cheese" as its direct object. In the next three examples the element of redundancy reappears, since these neuter nouns (fenum, bladum, corredium) have only one form ending in ...u-, - the ...um form. Nevertheless, the preceding cariare in every case announces these as direct objects (in the accusative case).

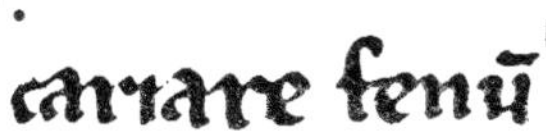 l.21  l.26 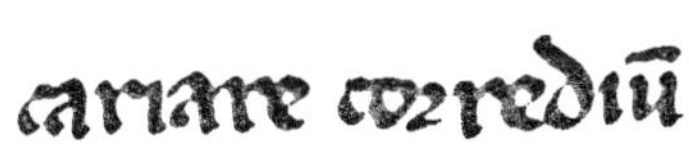 l.39

We may cheat a little here by introducing some examples freed of other, distracting problems:

inveniet seminatorē l.8 pascet illū l.33 facere mullon̄ l.22

As I have already admitted, this principle of inferring a nominative or an accusative by virtue of relationship to a verb still leaves open (in the case of an accusative) the question of number. In our examples, the object could be singular or plural:

seminatore**m** or seminatore**s**;   mullone**m** or mullone**s**.

Generally the sense of the passage leaves little doubt. As we have previously discovered, **-ē-** seems regularly to mean **-em-** (or **-en-**), so here it must be seminatore**m** in the singular. Of course illū can only be illu**m**, since the corresponding plural, illo**s**, is incompatible with illu-.

In principle, absolutely any grammatical relationship could be exploited as the means of deducing a suspended ending. For the present these three will suffice: the particular case expected after a particular preposition; the agreement of adjective with the noun it qualifies; the relation of verb with its grammatical subject and object.

To practise your grasp of these points, complete the suspended words in the following examples. In order to focus your attention on the essential details, I present them in transcribed form. By all means refer to the text (Text VI, page 7) if you want to see them unadulterated. Some appear in other chapters; the repetition is deliberate.

line 11. ad fest'
line 10. dabit .... ij den[ar]
line 9. averia .... quiet'
line 33. in cervis' [cervisia = ale]
line 3. pro unoquoque iugo bou' [unusquisque = every; iugum = yoke]
line 7. ducere sem [seed]
line 17. ad falces acuend
line 19. si dominus nullum cullard' haberet

Expanded versions of these examples are as usual in the Key (p.119).

Four Signs

Early in the previous chapter I advised you to "disregard obvious differences among the signs of shortening" that would appear in examples in that chapter. It is time now to address ourselves directly to this variability.

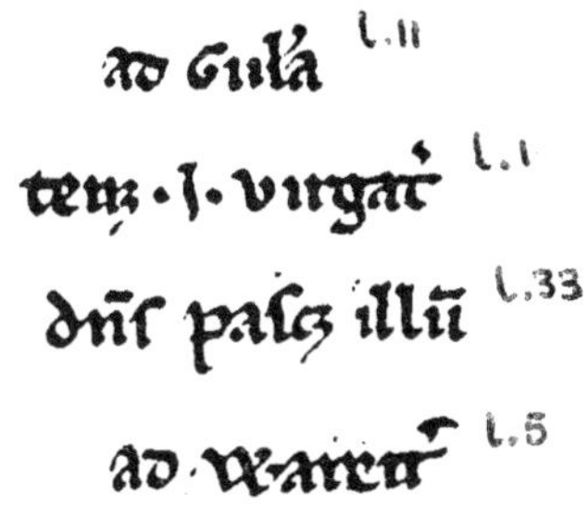

Look again at these: We see here the main means used by this scribe to mark shortenings of any kind. We have two ʒs, and four superscript signs: ʾ ʂ ‒ ʕ - the hook, the twist, the line and the flourish, we might call them. Like the letters of the alphabet, the signs are not uniformly written. The hook looks, when it is attached to a lower case **d**, as if it is a continuation of the curved stroke that forms the bowl of the **d** ( ), but instances of clear discontinuity of line show that it must be an additonal stroke ( ). The line, it must be noted, is apt to acquire a distinct curvature ( ). The fourth of them, the flourish, is hard to describe. I suggest it is best seen as the twist with an additional curve going from the top downwards to the right. The complete sign sometimes looks rather like a modern capital **D** in old-fashioned cursive handwriting.

It is worth drawing attention to the fact that these signs (here indicating suspension) work in more than one way, each sign being usable in every way. All four can be used to represent the complete grammatical suffix (virgat**am**, warect**am**), or just the final **m** (gula**m**, illu**m**), or the final **i** of a stem as well as the grammatical suffix (herbag**io**)[1]. It is not really profitable to generalise about which of the signs usually occurs in certain situations, since scribal practice simply is not uniform in this matter.

To prepare you for this variability, I offer now some practice in writing suspended words, arranged by the sign actually used by our scribe in particular cases. To help you I have eliminated other distracting signs and printed in **bold type** the point at which the relevant sign is to be supplied. This is an exercise in writing, not an opportunity to transcribe.

1. cf.p.119, the Key to the exercise overleaf.

line	twist	flourish	hook
val ob			vȝ ob
	9panag	9panag	
arura iiij bou	iugo bou		
bladu dni			fuit blad
mullon	multon		
correditu	i cur	i grang	i fald dni

For the scribe's version of these, see the Key (p.119). You will also find there, if you are curious, the expanded forms of these words.

This is a convenient place to mention a sign of suspension that was the origin of a famous misunderstanding, one that survives to this day. You will sometimes meet a roughly oblique line, usually somewhat curved, made through the last pen-stroke of a suspended word if that stroke is horizontal and roughly on the base-line. The only clear candidate for this treatment is the "round" or 2-like **r**. The commonest opportunity for such a suspension is, in fact, in genitives plural (-arum, -orum, -erum). Hence even Johnson and Jenkinson introduce the sign [ꝝ] under the label "-rum". Nevertheless, any suspension at **r** is capable of this treatment.

Very understandably, when scribes had to write the lengthy place-name Saresberia or its adjective Saresberiensis, they suspended at the earliest possible point, the **r**. They wrote, in either case, simply Saꝝ. Alas! Uninformed readers, used to the simple equation "ꝝ = -rum", read this as Sarum, and so Sarum became in popular belief the "old name" for Salisbury. By the same process Blandford Forinseca became "Blandford Forum".

Some problems of Suspension

In an earlier chapter we looked at some of the common grammatical clues with which the reader makes sense of words suspended by the scribe. I commented that any grammatical rule could serve the same purpose, and we find, for example, uses of the ablative without a preposition such as the ablative absolute. In our chosen text we find, too, examples of that notorious terror of school-students, gerundive attraction, as well as more straightforward gerundives to express obligation.

To take the "more straightforward" first, we meet twice the notion that the duration of a service will be determined by the amount of the lord's crop there is to reap or cart:

(a) dum bladum domini fuerit metend' l.23 (b) quamdiu fuerit cariand' l.26

In neither case is there any difficulty about supplying the ending of the suspended word: bladum appears as the subject of fuerit in (a), giving us metend**um**; bladum is also discovered to be the subject of (b) [see line 26 of the text] giving us cariand**um**.

Now for Gerundive Attraction. Torn from its context, 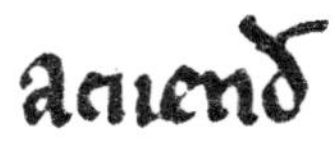 might have caused a little difficulty. But it appears as part of a rather specialised duty: 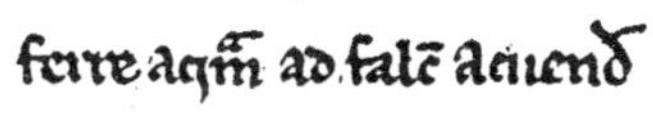 l.17

We can now use our already deciphered ferre aquam ("to carry water") to make sense of this. falc- means sickle, and acu- is of course to sharpen. We are left with two possibilities:

ad falc**em** acuend**am** or ad falc**es** acuend**as**.

Since the service is clearly a general one, the meaning will be unaffected by the question of singular or plural[1]. The service was to provide water for wetting the whetstone when sickles were sharpened.

---

1. For an instance where the plural is indicated by a preceding numeral see the footnote on page 51.

I have to admit, however, that every transcriber has in mind at least the possibility that someone may read the transcript. To print doubts and ambiguities is best avoided, if possible. Very often, your historical knowledge and your familiarity with the wider context from which your text has come will give guidance if not a definite resolution of the doubt. In this particular case a student would know of the survey made twenty years previously. In an entry concerning a different manor appears this same service and the published transcript has,

debet ferre aquam ad falces acuendas tempore falcationis

It is not easy to check the original manuscript of this text, but at least the reader wrestling with ad falc' acuend' has this version as well as the general sense to support a preference for the plural.[1]

Once again the novice may be surprised at the complexity of this discussion, but I hope that it is clear, and that its lessons will prove profitable. One of these should be that even forms that look advanced in terms of school Latin are tractable.

At the other extreme of suspended words are those where for one reason or another grammar is not a sufficient guide. Before we take the two main groups, I would emphasise that here as in other forms of word-shortening there is a comforting rule-of-thumb: scribes are most likely to shorten the words that occur most frequently, if only because they are most bored by the sight of them. So the novice must be prepared to postpone judgement on strange-seeming shortened words; the likelihood is that they will occur again and again, - in a less abbreviated form with a bit of luck. Recall the course of the discussion (p.27) of 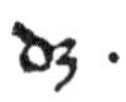 . Some abbreviations are so common that, as in English, we never meet them written in full. At least our scribe writes  , not , for scilicet.[1.14, 30, 34.]

The first group of suspensions is easily named: it consists of indeclinable words, - words whose form never changes, of which scilicet is the most obvious example. The second group comprises declinable words - and leaves the reader with the task not only of determining the ending of a word but also of identifying the word itself.

1. The MS removes any doubt: 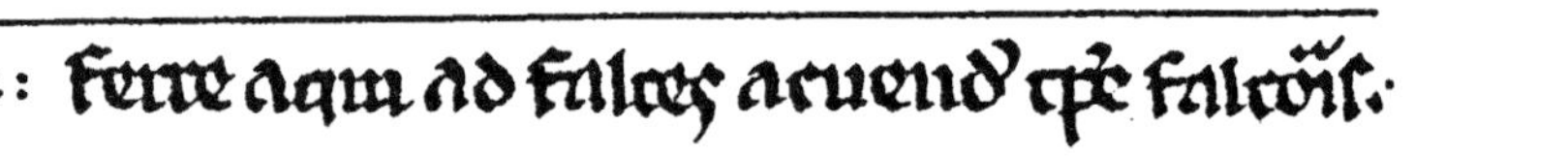

Consider these examples:

(1)  (4) 

(2)  (5) 

(3) 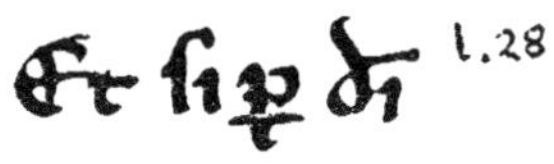 (6) 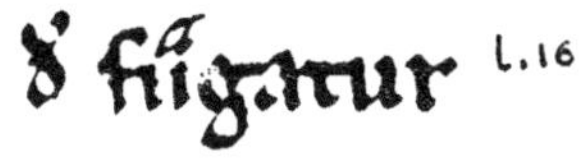

On the face of it, they are alike in including stumps or rumps of words, all beginning with d- , some consisting of nothing more than the **d** and the mark of shortening. Fortunately, in every case the context is helpful, especially to a reader who has some familiarity with this kind of text.

(1) With or without the valet ( ), v.d. presents no difficulty, especially as **d.**(penny) was still current until recent times. Admittedly, the full Latin denarius might not have sprung readily to the lips of every single user of pre-decimal currency, but in transcripts den. suffices.

(2) The confusing item ending pcar d' may be best clarified by looking two lines lower in the text (line 31), where we have the slightly fuller........... 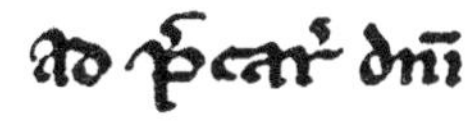

ad pcar dnī.

For our present purposes it is not necessary to disentangle the whole item. Evidently d' here stands for domini.[1]

(3) It would perhaps be a rather lazy reader who assumed that the di' after per was itself the noun 'governed' by per. Reading on to the next line we find the whole word diem, giving the phrase 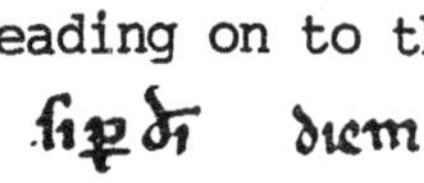 This suggests that di' is an adjective or something of the sort, qualifying diem. What that adjective might be becomes clearer when we pay attention to the full sentence: 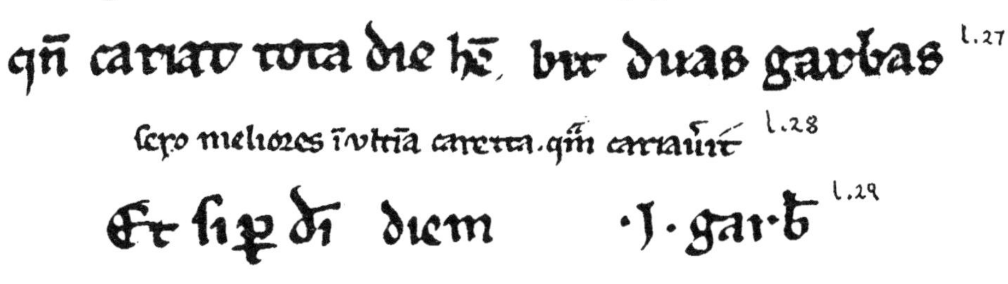

1. The inserted ij makes it ad ij precarias, not ad precariam.

Admittedly, what looks like a scribal error[1] makes confident interpretation of the sentence hazardous, but the phrase tota die is apparently contrasted with our per di' diem just as duas garbas appears to be contrasted with j garb. Some simple arithmetic lends support to the idea that di' means "half", dimidiam in Latin.[2]

(4) Armed with this new knowledge, you will not be daunted by di' acram.

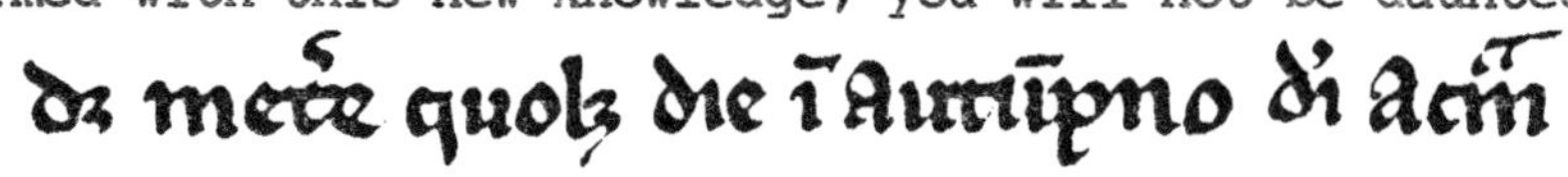

l.23

The clause from which it comes works well: "He has to reap, every day in autumn, a half acre."

(5) You are now primed to see every instance of di' as dimidiam, - a dangerous state of mind. However, the hypothesis is worth testing. Alas! The next example is made more complicated by the fact that the noun following our supposed dimidiam/dimidium (belatedly we remember that bonus-type adjectives have distinct masculine, feminine and neuter forms) is itself shortened.

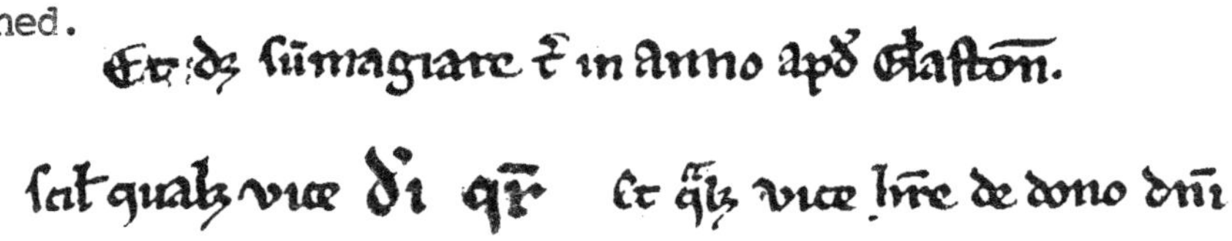

lines 34-5

What can be made of qr̄? The sentence runs thus: "He has to do pack-animal service three times a year to Glastonbury, that is to say, on each trip, half a ...., and on every trip to receive as the lord's gift ...." All we can suppose is that the obscure qr̄ represents a quantity or measure of the amount of service. Expressions of time and distance that could become qr̄ are hard to imagine, but, remembering that grain was likely to be among such burdens, the series Bushel, Quarter, Hundredweight comes to mind, at least, to older readers. Fine! qr̄ = quarterium, and the assigned load is half a Quarter, dimidium quarterium.

---

1. Surely totam diem (="for a whole day")? Conceivably our MS is a copy, and we have here a carelessly copied totā diē from which the copyist has omitted the sign ¯.

2. Half the number of sheaves for half a day's work - typically strict arithmetical proportionality in an estate such as this.

(6) Not for the first time the difficulties of the novice are aggravated by a word being split at the end of a line. Nor is our scribe a regular provider of the helpful medieval equivalent of the hyphen in this situation, a light oblique stroke. In my last example, d' frangatur, I am doubly unkind in so presenting it to the learner. The d' is the END of a word begun on the previous line. Let me put the bits together:

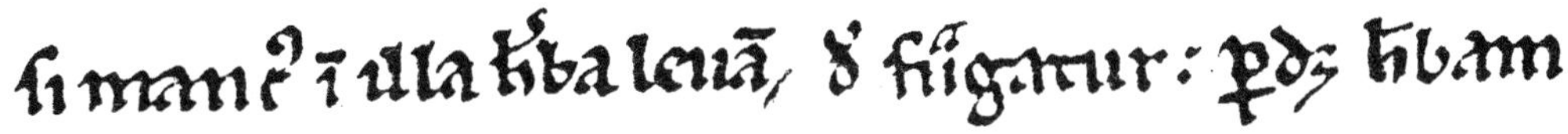

Still puzzled? Transcribing what we can, we have, si mancus in illa herba levand' frangatur, perdet herbam. The -and- rings a bell, brings back to mind, in fact,

 l.17

ad falces acuendas; so our example actually stands for in illa herba levanda. And the d' was a fraud - not the beginning of a word, but its (slightly shortened) ending.

In the course of these six analyses we have followed several approaches. Parallel passages have been useful, the meaning of the passage as a whole has been a guide, and we have leant on grammatical rules - even dealing easily with gerundive attraction. I hope that you have also learnt from my unkind snippets that it is wise to look beyond the immediate difficulty to see if the neighbouring words shed any light.

We now turn to another doubly obscure example, - not in order to intimidate you, but because multiple difficulties are all too common. Here in one fell swoop we have the two classes of difficult suspension juxtaposed (the declinable and the indeclinable): 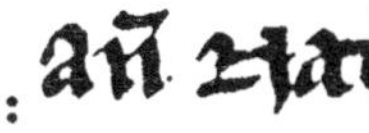 l.4

The problem is not made easier by the presence of a rather un-modern looking capital, in fact **N**. In the manuscript there follow two more shortened words, 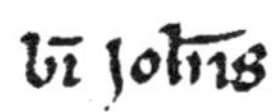 . The suspicion that we are dealing with a John, together with the immediately surrounding references to "days", suggests days relating to the feast of St John (or one of them!), - beati Johannis, in fact. Which feast? Nativitat- ("of the birth"), perhaps, and  would be ante. So, widening the context, we have the fifteen days next before the Birthday of the Blessed John. I fear that few novices would come so easily to that conclusion. When a novice, I did not. I work now from a wider experience. As explained, we have at times to postpone judgement and wait for enlightenment from later texts. The main point here is that Nat̊ is short for Nat-ivitat-em. The omitted portion contained part of the stem as well as the grammatical ending.

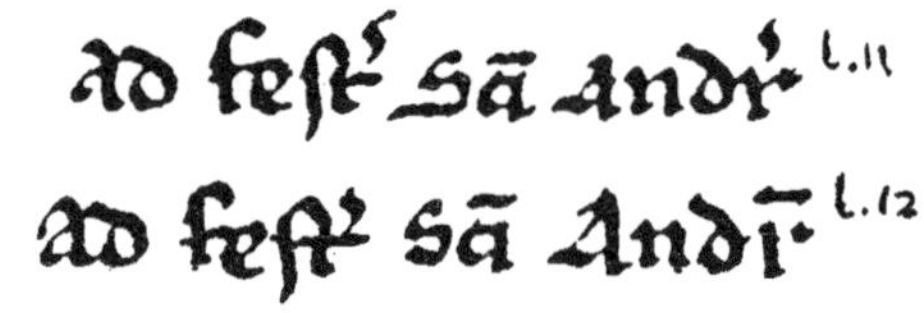

This discussion has prepared our minds for another feast day. ad festum, surely? And if bī was Beati, then perhaps Scī is Sancti.[1] The saint must be Andrew, Andreas in Greek (and also in Latin), with the Greek genitive Andree, a piece of information that is not likely to be on the tip of the novice's tongue, I fear. But Andr̄ must surely be Andrew.

The upshot of this discussion is that suspensions can be difficult. Fortunately, such examples are fairly rare. The principles I have been unfolding will, however, apply also to other kinds of shortening. But before we leave this last extract from the manuscript, we should note how the obviously identical expressions that I cited last differ slightly in the signs or marks used to mark suspension. Here we have clearly one feature for which the chapter "Not One For One" was preparing the ground. Two quite different signs mean the same thing: a bit chopped off. Even the fact that it is the SAME bit in each case does not preclude the use of different signs: .

I have introduced you now not only to signs but to other matters. It is time to re-vamp your notes, tackling at least these points:

SIGNS - different signs can serve the same purpose:

KINDS OF SUSPENSION - (a) tail-end of indeclinable words
(b) grammatical suffixes (or final letter of)
(c) end-chunk including part of stem & ending

KINDS OF CLUE - (a) grammatical - preposition + a particular case
- case-usage without preposition
- agreement (concord)
(b) meaning, esp. of neighbouring words

---

1. Strictly, bī, scī, and Johīs lie outside the scope of this chapter. It seemed silly to omit therefore the key examples. (See pages 64 - 65).

Contraction and Omission

You will have realised before this point that when we come to deal with words shortened by the omission of one or more bits from the middle we very seldom have the aid of grammatical clues. On the face of it, we are left with meaning as our sole guide; we have always to ask ourselves, "What would make sense here?"

I suggested earlier[1] that there is a rule of thumb, according to which the likelihood and the extent of shortening depend on the frequency with which the scribe is obliged to write the word in question. So the first step is always to cast around for a word that could be the shortened word in fuller form. In our discussion of ʒ we exploited the convenient presence of debent and debʒ to lead us to the meaning of dʒ.

At this point I should mention the useful habit of making different shortenings of the same word in close proximity, so that A provides a clue to B and B provides a clue to A. The following examples illustrate the practice:

l.7 

l.7 

These occur on a single line of our text (line 7). They are typical "different shortenings", but of course it is unlikely that you would have difficulty in recognising either version of acram on its own.

l.4 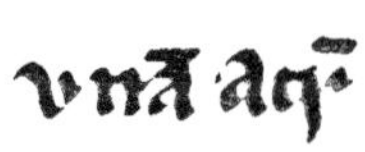

l.25 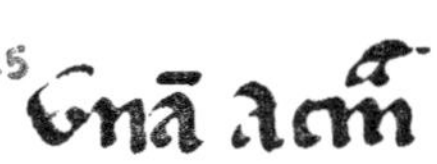

Surprisingly, there are only two other occurrences of acram on the page, but the scribe has found two more ways to write it. Of these four versions of acram, two are unusual. Analyse the shortening of each version, to discover exactly how it accords with the principles we have been studying. (see Key, page 120)

ex. 

ex. 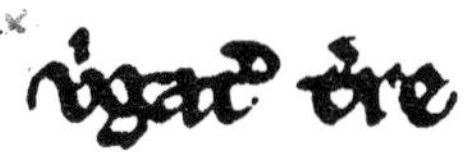

From the reverse folio come these apparent shortenings of virgat.. terre. The grammatical ending is not deducible from these de-contexted snippets.

ex. 

This (from the same source)[2] lends support to our surmise.

---

1. See page 50.
2. Compare the flourish over -at with virgat on line 1 of our text.

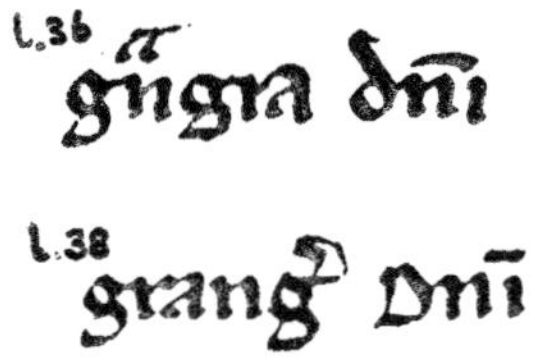

Once again a neat reciprocity. The usual interpretation of superscript **a**(^{a}) as -ra-[1] is confirmed in grang', and the general sign of suspension (the flourish ꝰ) is obligingly filled out for us in g^{a}ng**ia**.
Hence, gr**a**ng**ia** is the complete version of both.

That may appear to be something of a digression. It was intended to emphasise once more the vital principle enunciated in my first chapter: your Reference Book first, foremost, and nearly always is the manuscript text before you. Here its application is that the interpretation of a tricky word is often made easier because the scribe has written a variant of it nearby.

If that source of help fails, some readers have a sort of crossword-puzzle approach: "**s**-blank-blank-**c**-blank-**i**; something to do with John." We partly employed this method in our attack on an̄ Nat on pages 53-54. It is the clue to ſcd̃m (1.18), which must be **s**-e-**c**-un-**d**-u-**m**.

Usually less is omitted than in the case of **Nat**-ivitat-em, and guessing the blanks is not difficult. We have previously concluded that 9suetudie must be consuetudine. The context guides us, of course. We inferred that the object of "mow" must be "grass" or "meadow". Unfortunately, context sometimes fails to specify very tightly the limits of meaning. For example, the duty of a peasant to carry some object leaves wide open the nature of that object: cheese, fabric to make habits for the monks, the manorial rent, a mill-stone, ... In the rather repetitive content of many historical documents, it is the rare detail that sheds light. This very rarity means that guessing from the context is not enough. Any such guess must at least be compatible with the signs of shortening provided by the scribe, and prudent readers will squeeze help from the particular signs before committing themselves to a guess. In any case, some accidental error is unavoidable, and we should not increase the possibility of error by deliberately introducing loose or casual procedures.

---

1. Similarly, gnar̃ (line 6), a word we shelved on page 22, must begin granar-. On the analogy of lard̃ar̃ ,lardarium (line 2), granar**ium** is likely to be the full word.

So it is time to address ourselves directly to the particular signs of shortening, discovering which signs are capable of giving information about the omitted letters.

We have already become accustomed to the superscript  as probably meaning -ra- (or -ua- after **q**). It seems possible to suppose that this sign is a reduced (and garbled) **a**. That is to say, it preserves in its use as a sign the essential **a** from which it was derived.[1] In line with this is the use of actual, identifiable letters in the superscript position to indicate that the omission includes that particular letter. See if you can fill in the blanks in the following:

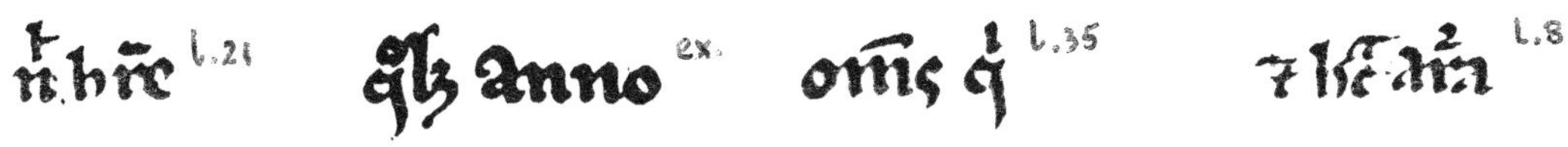

____ habere   ____ libet anno   omnes ____   et ____ ar ____ [2]

The use of superscript letters is slight compared with the use of less familiar signs. The next two chapters deal with the commonest of these apparently abstract or non-representational signs.

---

1. The normal unqualified reference to it as "superscript **a**" disregards the head that characterised lower case **a** in many medieval hands ().
2. See Key for confirmation of your completion of these items.

The Twist

Our main concern is with marks that have no obvious relation to letters and have as one of their functions the non-specific signal, "Here letters have been omitted." The question is whether any of them can be shown to have a reliably predictable specific use. In our scribe's hand (and many others) there is one mark or sign that so often appears where a particular pair of letters is dropped that one may say, "It generally stands for ... ." We have already skirted round it in the course of other analyses. We shall now come to grips with this mark by concentrating on another of those balanced sentences that can be so helpful:

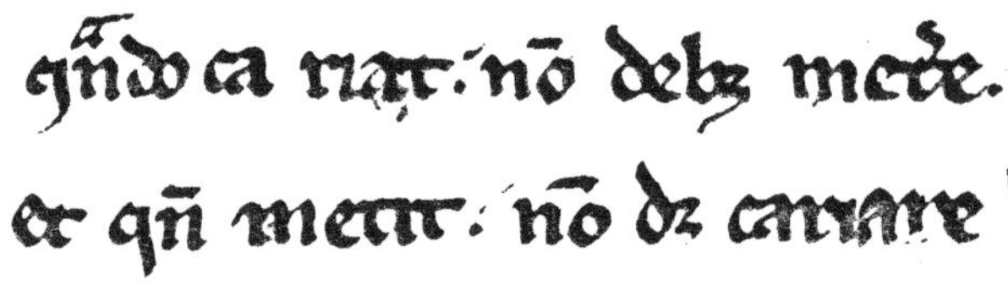
lines 26-27

We have already tackled parts of this, but it will pay to highlight the parallelism:

	quando	cariat	nō	debʒ	me^{s}te
et	qn̄	metit	nō	dʒ	cariare

Making use of previous gains, this becomes

	quando	cariat	non	debet	me^{s}te
et	qn̄	metit	non	debet	cariare

Only the most reluctant detective could resist the conclusion that, here at least, qn̄ represents quando and that me^{s}te must be an infinitive, specifically the infinitive of meto from which we have metit in line 2. This is metere. Once again we have laboriously, but irresistibly, come to the meaning of a sign: ^{s} here signifies -er-.

You may well already have turned back to inspect some of the little extracts examined in Text XV. At that point occurred the suggested metere (infinitive) after a shortened version of debet. A little searching provides the following, from which we can extract the infinitives alongside them:

l.7  ducere

l.22  facere

l.38  fieri

Text XV included other relevant material, however. We met the phrase 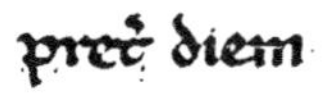 : "Could be the preposition preter + acc." Indeed, what else could it be? So the twist can mean -er in completing a suspension. It is not just for mid-word omissions, nor is it confined to verbs. It is time for another methodical search. From our single page of text emerge the following; students are invited to transcribe them unassisted:[1]

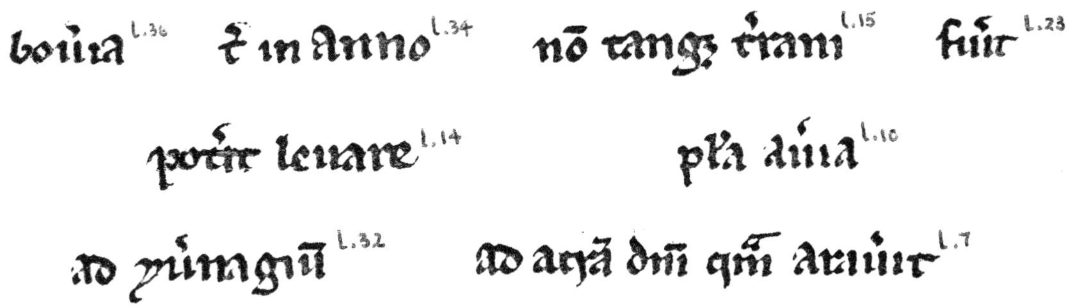

Conveniently, our search brings to light another pair of parallel passages: (a) 

(b) 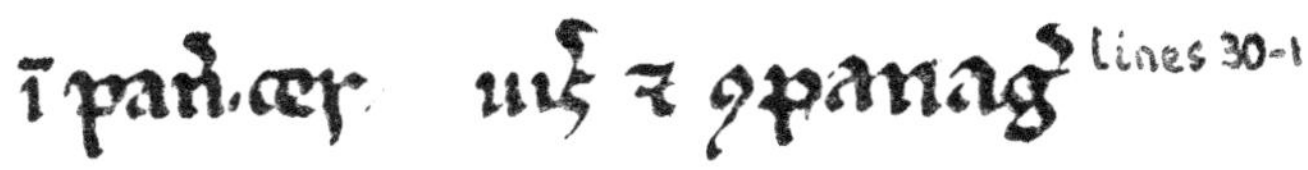

The parallelism is obscured in the manuscript because in the second version a word is interrupted at the end of a line. Not just any word, but the word on which we need to focus. Remembering that the (suspended) in is followed by the ablative case, we can expand these lines:

in pane cervisio et companagio

The fully written syllable cer- in (b) confirms our reading of the twist above c in (a).

Still convinced of the value of practice, I invite you now to write these words in our scribe's hand, using the twist for -er-, and also introducing any other common signs of shortening that seem appropriate:

Wynterborn; debent bis commedere; iiij averia cum bobus domini.

In the Key you will find the scribe's version.

So far, so good. However, a thorough search also reveals this little

---

1. See key for transcriptions.

collection:

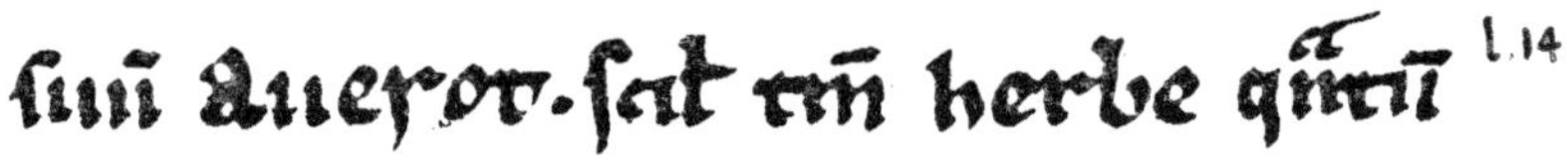

At once we see - if we had not gathered as much previously - that -er- is not invariably represented by the twist. Here we have herbe in full, herba with the twist, and herbam with the superscript line. Similarly the page contains two versions of herciare (to harrow), one with the twist and one with the line.

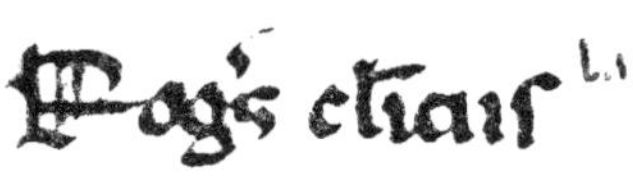

It is easy to overlook the obvious, like Roger the Clerk, for instance! Two signs for -er- again.

Finally, we remind ourselves of the feast of St.Andrew:

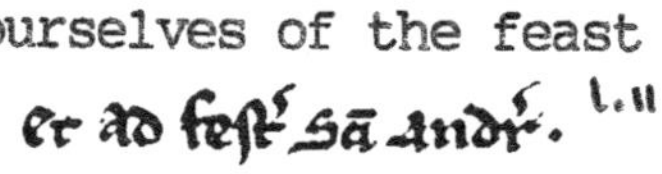

Here the twist is twice used, not for -er, but simply as a non-specific sign of suspension[1]. This was how we first classified it (pages 47-8).[2]

This discussion has been fairly exhaustive, necessarily. How best to think about this matter is not a question to be answered by someone with experience simply laying down the law; the learner needs to arrive at an answer through careful consideration of as much evidence as can be readily assembled.

Among points you may like to consider is the question of what letter or letters commonly precede the omitted -er-. Our sample is small, but in both verbs and nouns we find a number of cases of **-ver-**, the **v** being usually represented by **u**. Are there other letters frequently occurring before the **-er-**? Is there a pattern in the decision to omit or to use the twist?

---

1. For slightly divergent views of which came first, the specific or the non-specific use of the twist, see L.C.Hector, The Handwriting of English Documents (p.31), and C.Johnson & H.Jenkinson, English Court Hand (p.59).
2. We also twice met  (on p.51). Without comment I transcribed this as pre-. This is regular usage. See p.85 (E) for supporting evidence.

The Superscript Line

In the last few pages I have taken you through a careful discussion of one of the marks that have no obvious relation to letters and have as one of their functions the non-specific signal, "Here letters have been omitted." Together we tackled the question whether the twist could be shown to have a reliably predictable specific use. It is time now to look systematically at the other common sign of shortening, the superscript line. After your first piece of detective work I suggested that a line over a vowel (especially at word-ends) possibly represents **-m-**, and later it emerged that we should consider **m** and **n** as alternative meanings. In the course of our study of suspension we found that the superscript line was one of the four marks used by our scribe to indicate suspension of a word. So this sign has both specific and non-specific uses. Can we now fill in this broad picture with the details? How is the novice to approach the numerous occurrences of this sign in our text?

My approach here will be to provide first a systematic survey of the varied uses of the sign, and only then to suggest probabilities and priorities. If you are shy of formal classification, skip to page 66. I must stress to you that experience will work wonders, and much that seems to need careful consideration now will seem painless one day. I propose that we first focus on the position of the superscript line. Does it lie above a vowel, above a consonant or vaguely above two or three letters? The last-named class consists of a small number of mostly familiar words (in the given context), words whose shortening is special in another sense, - and so to be kept till last.

I Line-over-a-vowel

I-A WHERE THE COMPLETION IS BEYOND DOUBT.
It is reassuring to discover that in many instances there can be no doubt what must be supplied by the reader when the scribe marks a shortened word with the superscript line above a vowel. There are at least three ways in which such certainty can arise.

I-Ai First, there are words whose form never varies (a small class in Latin), words which you will readily identify by the residual letters.

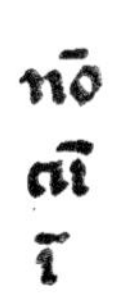

We have met all these previously, and you will doubtless notice at once that the full forms of these examples end in either **m** or **n**.

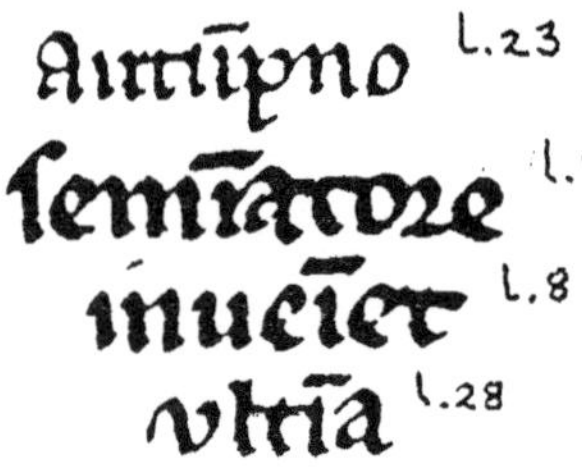

I-Aii The next group comprises words capable of inflection (i.e. with variable endings). It is from the stem or unchanging part of these words that a letter has been dropped. Usually such words are quite long and can be readily identified.[1] Unfortunately, we meet here the first jarring note in an otherwise fairly harmonious system.

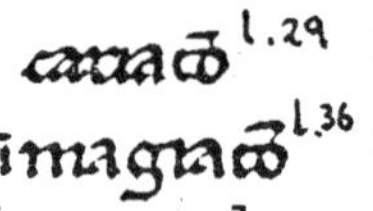

[summag-]

In our now well-trodden page of text we have two examples in which the missing letter could not conceivably be "m or n". At this point we could easily become bogged down in a discussion of the consonant immediately preceding the marked vowel. Needlessly. Suffice it to say that  signifies -cio or -tio. The difference is entirely without significance, but -cio seems to be the preferred rendering these days.

I-Aiii The third group of shortened words where there can be no doubt about the completion comprises all neuter nouns in **-um** (like bellum). Our scribe writes 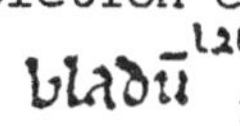, 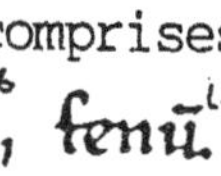, and (tidied up for you) pratū.[l.12] The point is that in the declension of these nouns the only form ending "**u** blank", as crossword puzzlers say, is **-um**. Remember:

bell-**um**, bell-**um**, bell-**um**, bell-i, bell-o, bell-o;

bell-a, bell-a, bell-a, bell-orum[2], bell-is, bell-is.

The alert reader have noticed that once again **m** had to be supplied. It may by now also begin to be apparent that this is not necessarily because some quality in **m** makes it suitable for omission. We simply need to bear in mind the fact that the letter **m** occurs with indecent frequency in the endings of nouns and adjectives, and barely less frequently in verbs.

---

1. See Key.

2. The ending of bellorum is -orum. No suspension of bellorum could produce bellū. As we saw on p.48, -rum usually appears as 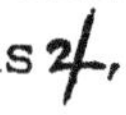, hence the suspended version would be 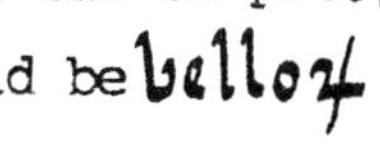.

It is time for more practice. Try your hand at writing in our scribe's hand the following words, shortening them by omission and then inserting the superscript line. (Other shortenings may occur to you.)

eandem summagiare consuetudine levandam corredium[1]

I-B GRAMMATICAL COMPLETION.

Many readers will be confident with the limited selection of grammatical endings commonly encountered in medieval texts. For them there should be certainty about the completion of another set of words whose shortening is marked by the superscript line. We have touched on this matter before, but it will bear further mention. Simply, the ending of many words is left beyond doubt thanks to the rules of grammar.

I-Bi We find instances of the line above a vowel at the end of a noun following a preposition. As we noted above, such suspended words could, in principle, be either singular or plural, but not here.

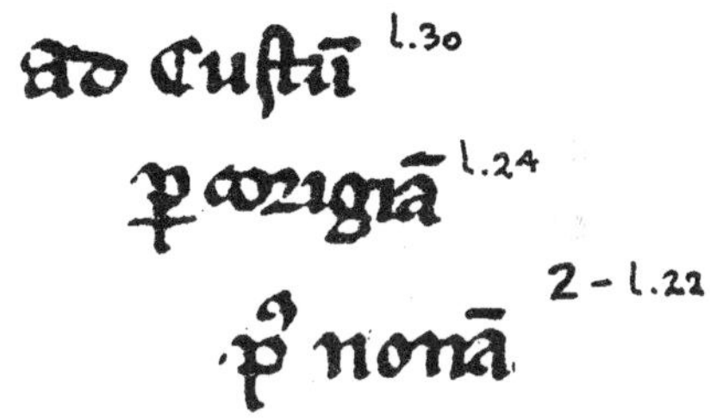

I-Bii

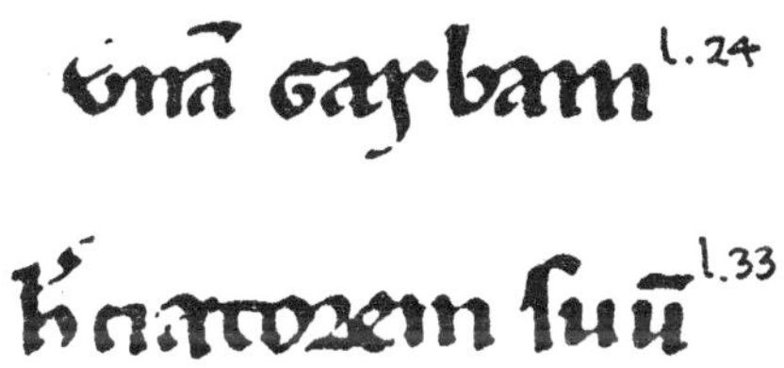

Then there are the cases where a word clearly agrees with its neighbour in the grammatical sense; we apply the rules of concord, especially the rule whereby an adjective agrees with its noun in case, gender, and number. The inexperienced student will be reminded by the second of these examples that agreement does not entail rhyme (<u>-orem</u>/<u>suum</u>).

I-Biii Finally in this section we find instances where the case of a noun or pronoun is determined by grammar even without a preposition; the word in question is either demonstrably the subject or object of a verb, or it is a dependent genitive (not illustrated here).

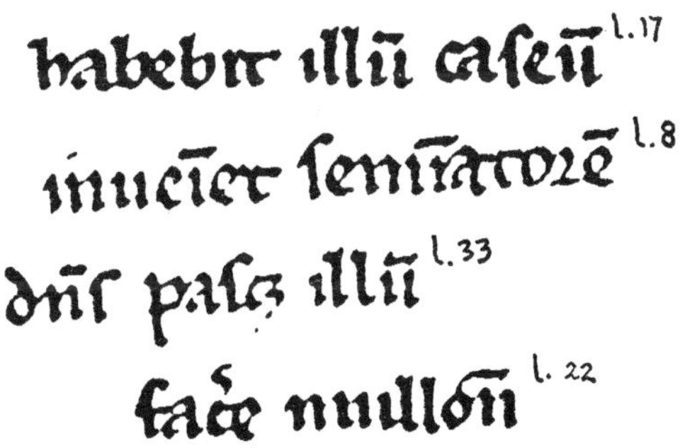

---

1. See Key.
2. I will come clean.  is a unique use of 9, and means <u>post</u>.

I-C EXPERIENCE IS NECESSARY

So far our discussion of a line-over-a-vowel has dealt with omission and suspension. Contraction brings us to the villains. We have already met two of these: bī [l.4](see p.53) dī [l.28](see pp.51-2) mīa [l.16]

Here we remember the rule of thumb, and hope that familiarity or frequency will save us.[1] We have seen elsewhere that **bī** is always beati, and that **dī** is probably dimidium/dimidiam. **mīa** occurs seldom in this text, but it can possibly be worked out from the context. We read that a mower's perquisite is as much hay as he can lift on the handle of his scythe. It is implied that greed might tempt him to overload the tool in question, causing it to break. If so, he is to lose the hay, perdet herbam. But null alia **mīa** pertinet. "No other .... applies" (or appertains). Penalty, surely? And the word in medieval Latin for penalty or fine is that most piquant of euphemisms, misericordia (pity). Now you see why I kept this sub-section till last.

II Line-over-a-consonant

When we come to the superscript line written above a consonant, we have to face up to a complication. We have seen that the mark above a vowel usually signifies that some matter that should follow has been omitted. The same mark above a consonant has wider possibilities: the matter omitted can lie BEFORE .... or AFTER the marked consonant, or BOTH:

sem[e]l̄ [2, l.33]   scil̄[icet] [2, l.34]   q[ua]n̄[do] [l.27]

(I shall follow this lay-out in sub-section Aii below.)

Again I must remind you that the rule-of-thumb applies: scribes tend to do the more drastic things to the more familiar words, and none of these three shortened words is likely to present a problem.

II-Ai Within this threefold framework the same general principles apply to consonants as to vowels. My three examples above correspond to my first example when we dealt with the line-over-a-vowel (non, cum, in), "words whose form never varies".

II-Aii We next dealt with letters dropped from the stem or unchanging part of inflected words, words with variable endings (autumpno, seminatore etc).

---

1. A longer skeleton occurs in cū.i.hoīe [l.37] ii.hoīes [l.29]. Surely homine/s?
2. Letters with 'ascenders' are often cut by the horizontal line: [...]

There are comparable examples associated with the line-over-a-consonant:

[BEFORE the mark]	[AFTER the mark]	[BEFORE and AFTER the mark]
d[omi]n̄i [l.2]	h̄[er]bam [l.15]	s[an]c̄[t]i [l.12]
seq[ue]n̄ti [l.6]	ip̄[s]e [l.35]	q[ua]r̄[ter...] [l.35] [1]
	sabb̄[at]i [l.24]	f[a]c̄[tu]s [l.17]

You will notice that some of these are easily identified, such as ipse, sequenti and even sancti. Dn̄i, of course, is as familiar as the sign for et. Herba is also fairly common, and occurs as we have seen in various disguises, easily seen through thanks to the context. We saw an instance of this previously in the discussion of mīa (p.64). I gave you the expanded perdet herbam, at once deducible from 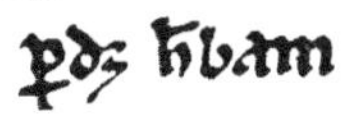 after the preceding text.

II-B Our final category in strict parallel with the line-over-a-vowel is when the completion of a suspended word is made safe by grammatical considerations. You will be relieved to find that here we have to deal with the line-over-a-consonant only when it indicates the omission of matter that should follow it. The three kinds of grammatical help are still available:

II-Bi per an̄n[**um**] [l.1] / in quinden[**a**] [l.5] } (noun follows preposition)

II-Bii ad festum sancti Andr̄[**ee**] [l.11] (concord)
ad illas delib̄[erand**as**] [l.37] (concord - plus a necessary insertion)

II-Biii si dominus nullum cullard̄[**um**] haberet [l.19] (direct object)

The last example reminds us of the principle of redundancy. Even without the supporting clue of nullum we should recognise[2] cullard- as the object of haberet.

* * * * * *

So much for my "systematic overview". What strategies are available to the reader actually encountering word-shortenings marked by this

---

1. See page 52 for a discussion of the required grammatical ending of qr.
2. We should, or rather we would, if both approaches (concord, verb-object relationship) were not made more difficult by the shortening of both nullum and haberet (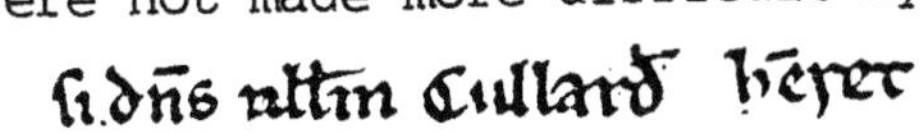)

versatile superscript sign? From various remarks you may already have gathered the chief strategies:

1. Look for a vowel beneath the sign; there is a strong chance that the sign represents **m** or **n**
2. If **m** or **n** seems wrong, or if the sign is above a consonant, regard the superscript line as non-specific. Treat it like any other non-specific mark:
   (a) make the most use you can of grammatical indicators;
   (b) neglect at your peril the sense of the passage in general and the particular meaning of the words adjacent to your present focus;
   (c) run mentally down your check-list of Commonly Occurring Words - you may be facing yet another variant of one of them.
3. Put the offending item on the back burner, into cold storage, or wherever you stow matters to which you hope to return. Indeed, it is best not to wrestle too strenuously on first encounter with a difficulty. So much becomes clearer after you have read on further...
4. In your early days, be tentative; use a pencil whenever there is the slightest doubt about your interpretation.

I can no longer postpone tackling the most chameleon-like of words in our text, the verb *habeo* in all its manifestations. Our scribe has to write many grammatical forms, even subjunctives, of this verb, and cavalierly shortens this already short stem (*hab-*) to ***h-***. He also wobbles in his treatment of any **e** that occurs, such as the first **e** of the infinitive, writing sometimes *hr̄e* and sometimes *hēre*. He is also content to omit one of the required signs of shortening, so that 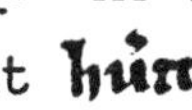 L.11 stands not for *huerit* but for *habuerit*. You have been warned. Seriously, once you have become used to this variability you will be ready to face other similarly varying manifestations. The verb "to be" (*sum*) naturally has challenges for the novice, though in our chosen text we have only one form, *fuerit*. This is once written out in full, and thrice shortened, with the twist to indicate the loss of ***-er-***:  L.17...

 Now transcribe these longer extracts: 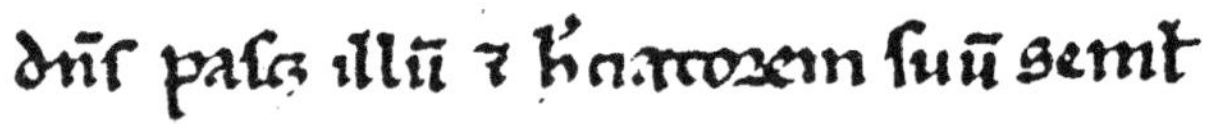 L.33

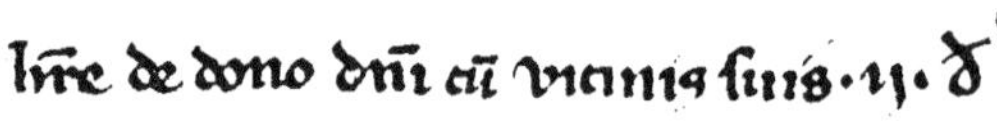 L.35 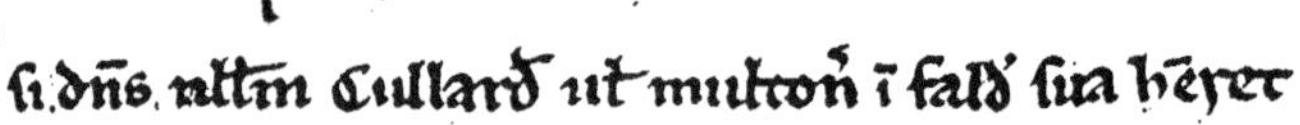 L.19

 L.23

Capital Matters

CAPITAL LETTERS AND .... LETTERS

I must preface this chapter with a point about terminology. Among the gaps in English, one that arises here is the lack of an unambiguous and unobjectionable opposite to 'capital'. One authority[1] refers to "ordinary letters", but that seems to me to ascribe an extraordinary status to capitals, whereas they are legitimate, in their place. 'Minuscule' sounds better, since the word 'minuscule' is regularly to be encountered for a kind or manner of lettering in contrast to 'majuscule' in which capital letters were predominant. Minuscule instantly suggests ancient writing hands. Unfortunately, its current use to denote non-capital letters seems mostly confined to specialists. Then there is the harmless and apparently obvious expression 'small letters'. I prefer to avoid this, since (as we shall see) medieval scribes often wrote small-sized capital letters. The opposite of this practice is the large size of non-capital **a**, to which I drew your attention on page 11(fn.). In modern educated usage, 'lower case' is perfectly clear and acceptable. True, it derives from the cases in which a compositor kept his letters, in the printing trade, but it is pressing literalism too far to exclude the term because of its origin. On that basis we could not call a betrothed couple (or an occupied toilet) ´engaged`, since no gauntlet is thrown down these days. So, **lower case** it shall be.

* * * * * *

The paucity of capital letters in our chosen text has led us to postpone the question of their decipherment so far, and this may have been something of a kindness to the novice. The fact is that capital letters can be easier than lower case letters, and they can be harder. A capital letter, like a lower case letter, can resemble some quite different letter. There is also the problem caused by varying forms of a single letter. Furthermore, we have at times no way of

---

1. English Court Hand, A.D. 1066-1500, Charles Johnson and Hilary Jenkinson (Oxford 1915)

being sure whether what we see is in fact a capital letter or not; the two are practically identical. The classic example is **K / k**, which Johnson and Jenkinson admit to be "often barely distinguishable". Then there is a new difficulty: medieval scribes were less rule-bound than we are about the use of capitals. Capital letters spring up in unexpected places, and they are absent when you might expect them to be present. Finally, in the nature of things capitals occur very much less often than lower case letters. This means that we have less opportunity to meet them, to learn by experience. Yet, in the end, it is the experienced eye that is needed to make sense of an obscure or elaborate capital.

I can offer you some solace. Essentially, the habits you have been acquiring are also those that you need for dealing with tricky capitals. By now it should be habit with you to consult the text itself, to search for comparable instances for help. You will also be in the habit of exploiting to the full any examples about which there can be no doubt - or little. You will also by now have some skill in identifying, and in attending to, significant detail in the shape of a letter. Granted the medieval fondness for elaborating capital letters, this last is especially important. Finally, on the bonus side, capital letters generally stand out boldly, with the result that searching for parallels is a great deal easier.

Let us now build up some confidence by contemplating straightforward capitals[1]: a set entirely without shortenings, and a set with some simple shortenings[2]:

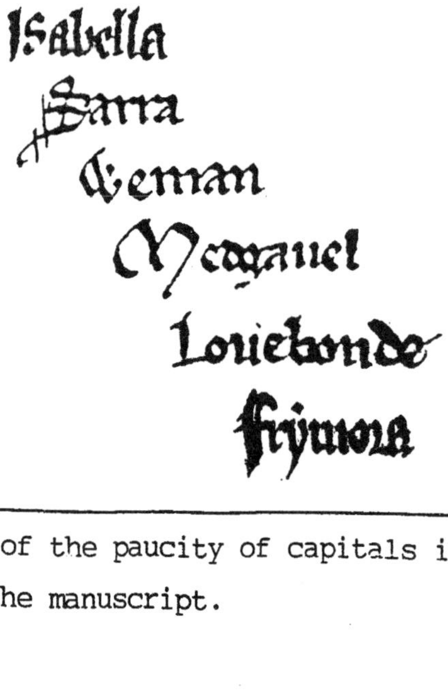

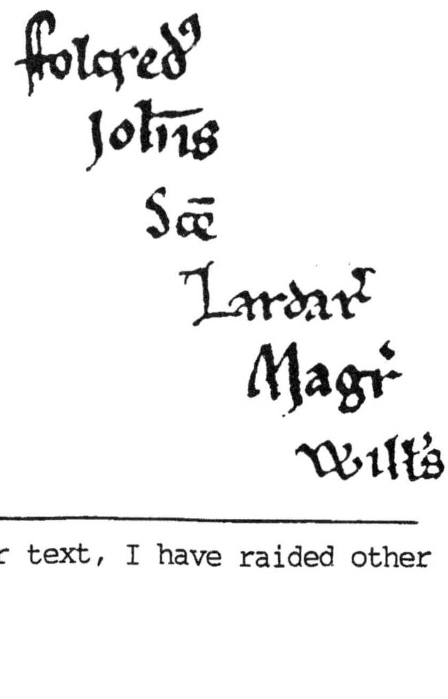

1. Because of the paucity of capitals in our text, I have raided other folios from the manuscript.

2. See Key.

Of course, a complete name or word can still baffle us, if it is unfamiliar, as names often are. To the novice technical terms are also a mystery, and scribes were apt to begin with a capital if the term was English, not Latin, as often happened when some ancient right was under discussion. We will proceed, therefore, with examples that are unlikely to be familiar to you.

Before wrestling with the capitals, transcribe the lower-case letters. You will have no trouble with -stcumbe, I imagine, but the second word is made harder by the dubious minims and the two signs of shortening. You ought to tumble to the second half, -cumbe (remember the superscript line over a vowel), and of course recognise that the two words have the same ending. They seem to begin alike, as well, but that's the rub. What letter begins each word, and what about those minims?

Following our custom, we search our source material for help. I shall make things easier for you by doing the search, Here are other items from that part of the MS with capitals that are more or less like our pair:

Clearly, the trick is knowing when other items are relevant. The rule must be: When in doubt, use it. If on later inspection an item seems after all to be unconnected with your search, jettison it.

What are we to make of this collection? Once again, transcribe the lower-case letters, and look to see what capitals would possibly make sense in each instance. You will quickly decide that among the set are Eodem, Emma, and Osmundus, and possibly you will also recognise Et and Osb[ertu]s. Former struggles (see p.110) declare Oportet, and from Trice Martin's useful "Record Interpreter" we confirm Eularia as a forename. So the array includes **Es** and **Os**. Some could be E **or** O. All have a roughly circular frame and one or more diameters. Our research has been inconclusive.

What about our cumbes, then? **O** or **E**? **E**stcumbe for the first has topographical probability (east-combe), but, replacing the twist by -er-, **O**ver- and **E**ver- seem equally possible prefixes for the second.[1]

Finally, it may be useful to reassemble our collection in a sequence where the vital differences appear progressively.

You will notice certain points:

1. It is exceptional for **E** to be based on a complete circle, and for **O** NOT to be so based.

2. **E** always has a horizontal, **O** does so seldom, if ever.

I propose to leave our favoured manuscript now for a brief diversion. There is a small text in a manuscript at Trinity College, Cambridge[2], written in a hasty, cursive hand, that deals, like our main text, with the affairs of Glastonbury Abbey. It gives in rare detail the exact shares in the meadow at Kennard's Moor held by various named individuals and officials of the abbey. Consequently, there are plenty of capitals. Sampling this text will enable you to consider at one blow both the effects of a different style of writing and the importance of attention to detail.

A tenant with more than one share in the meadow appears here:

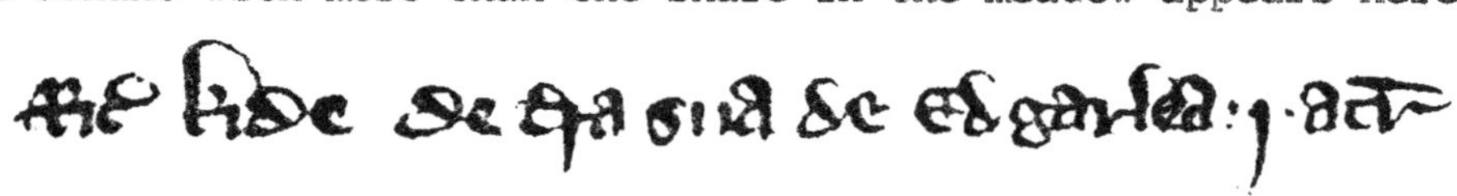

---

1. There is an Overcombe on the borders of Somerset and Dorset, rather distant from the manor of Deverel in which this place was found. However, in a village linked with this manor there is now a cottage called Boar's Bottom, near the foot of a combe. Ever- meant boar. Those who like circumstantial detail may see here a relic of **E**vercumbe.

2. Trinity College MS R.5.33, folios 116v and 117r.

Who is this man that here is said to hold "1 acre [of meadow] of his own land of Edgarlea"? The first name ends with a **c** and a twiddle, obviously a shortening. The second ends with -de. There is a marked resemblance between the two seeming initial capitals, except that the second has a magnificently elevated head. Let us seek out the other references to this wealthy meadow-man:

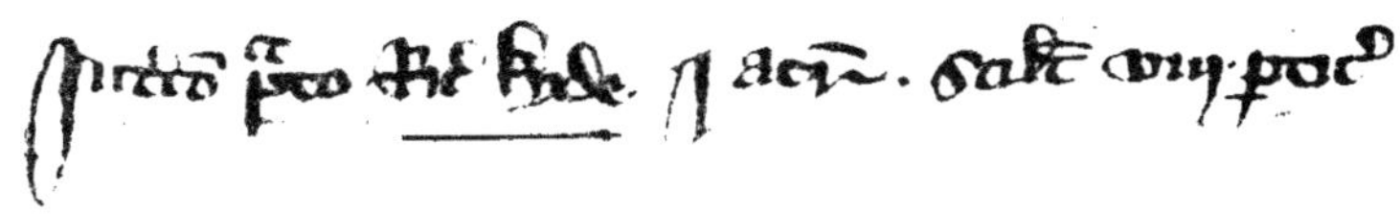

On close inspection we see (especially in the final example) that we may have an **i** immediately after the capital and before the endings that I identified, in both names. We also note that in each case the second name begins with the distinctive tall head, suggesting that this name begins with a different capital from the first name. This feature is consistently different, despite other points of similarity. That puts the first capital in a new light. Let us boldly represent this capital by a **bold** asterisk: *****ic'. This will make more profitable our now overdue search for other names with the same beginning. It yields the following group of tenants:

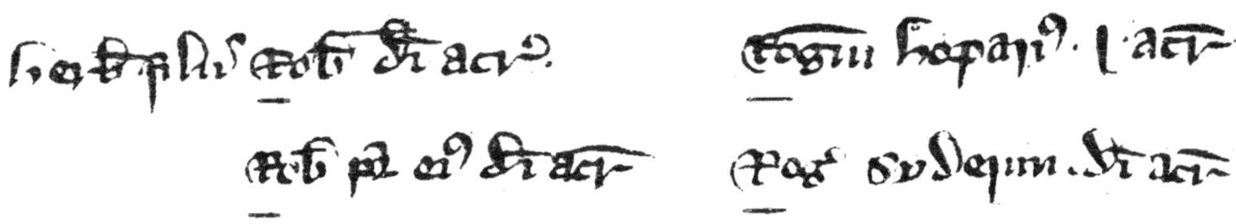

As usual, let us transcribe the lower-case letters. We have then :

herb' filius *****ob' di' acram   *****og.. hoparius j acram

*****ob' pr[?] eius di'acram   *****og' Syderun di' acram

Eliminating irrelevancies, we have these forenames: ***ic' *ob'** and ***og'**. Mindful of the frequent occurrence in medieval texts of modern forenames, we have no choice but settle for **R** as the asterisk. The names are Ricardus, Robertus, and Rogerus.

But what of the surname? What is the initial if it is not **R**? Unfortunately we have no comparable specimens on which to build. What can we deduce from the actual form of the letter? The tall head is certainly obtrusive, so perhaps it is a letter which is invariably high: **b d h k l.** Which? The complete bowl on the right of the down-stroke, well above the line, reminds us strongly of modern cursive **k**. The difference from modern cursive **k** lies in the angle of the tail; this medieval letter has a horizontal tail whereas ours descends obliquely to the line. Since this feature occurs in all three examples, we may as well conclude provisionally that the letter is in fact a **k**, and that the gentleman's name is **Ricardus Kide**. Like all our deductions, this must be with a mental note that later encounters may force us to reconsider our conclusion.

If we return now to our manorial survey, what instances can we find of this letter? There are four possible candidates in folios close to our text:

The two versions of Kingheswere certainly dispose of the problem of the angle of the tail. Scrutiny reveals a variability in its angle, from the horizontal of Kalston to the modern-looking oblique stroke of the thicker Kingheswere. So that although Kalston may be unfamiliar, and Koc a little surprising, we seem now to have a clear idea of at least the main features of capital **K**.[1]

Before we leave this enquiry, we should check also the kind of capital **R** to be found in our manorial survey.

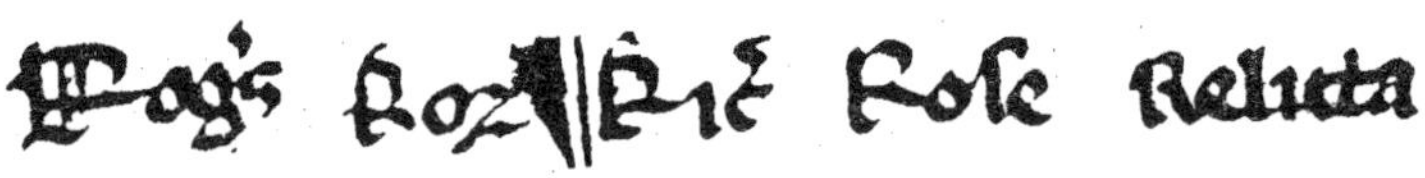

I leave you to examine these samples and to discover the very interesting parallels and differences between this **R** and the capital **K** of our main text, and also to identify the **R** that most nearly resembles the **R** of the cursive hand. You will notice a feature present in the cursive **R** that is at best vestigially present in this collection.

We began our research into capitals with a pair of "confusibilia", to borrow L.C.Hector's[2] useful term. There are others. When you meet a doubtful capital, you have to struggle. The context provides uncertain help with proper nouns, nor can you entirely rely on the scribe's provision of parallel examples. A medieval scribe would cheerfully write different spellings for the same name on consecutive lines. All you can do is acquire as clear a knowledge as possible of the key characteristics of each letter.

---

1. You may be interested to see one other **K** from the Trinity College text, - the name of the meadowland: 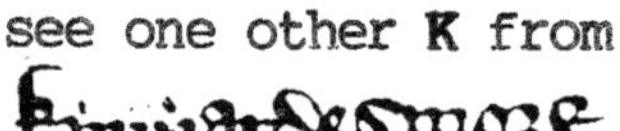
2. L.C.Hector, The Handwriting of English Documents.

If you carried out the writing exercises earlier in this book you will have found this a useful way of learning the vital details of lower case letters. It is time to do the same with capitals. I suggest you make your own notes on the "key characteristics" that help differentiate between confusibles, and then make your own alphabetical list of capitals. I offer here from our manuscript some samples of the chief offenders in this matter of confusibility.

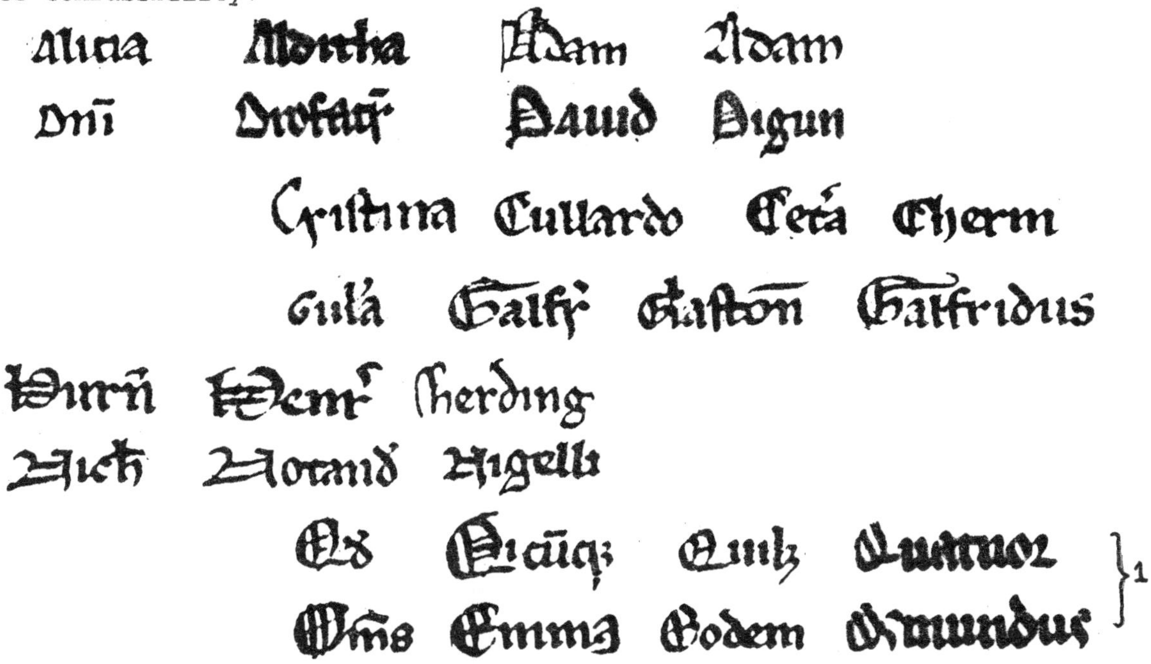

And here are examples of the less troublesome capitals - apart from those already appearing above.

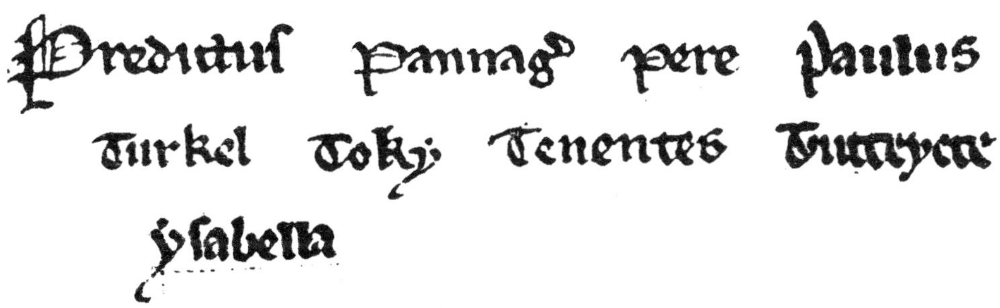

---

1. There are **three** confusibilia here.

Although my examples in this chapter have come mainly from a single text (not necessarily from a single scribe), there has been a surprising degree of variability in the letter-forms. This is true of the common capital that I omitted from my presentation of examples, the letter **B**.

I postponed this letter for a reason. In the cursive hand which provided material for the diversion above, **B** is particularly troublesome. It may be a salutary experience for you to face this letter now. The last of the series seems pretty remote from the earlier instances, but careful study will show how it arose.

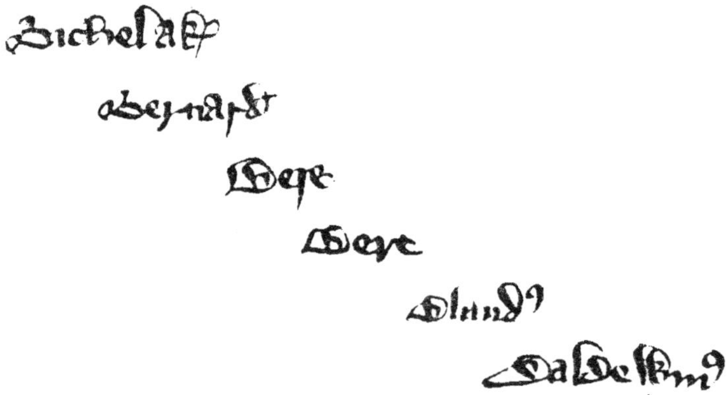

Pen Strokes

Our scribe writes in a formal, bookish hand, doubtless copying from an existing text (even if that was some less polished version of the material). He makes occasional mistakes, but his lettering is careful and well-formed. Nevertheless, even he is capable of presenting difficulties to the novice by the way his pen-strokes are made. What do you make of these items?

(a)  l.37 (b)  l.1

In these and similar specimens we meet the first such difficulty, one that can assume formidable proportions in other hands. It seems prudent, therefore, to address this problem while it is of manageable size.

It is a matter of **minims**. The letters **i**, **m**, **n**, and **u** were composed simply of vertical strokes (minims) duly provided with serifs at top and tail: 

The result can be a row of minims, no use being made of clear link and clear separation to distinguish one letter from another, still less to help their identification[1]. It is co-incidental that the classic example of the problem is the word "minimum" itself, which, written in full, consists of nothing but minims: 

Here are further samples from our text:

(c)  l.2 (d)  l.37

Two questions face us. Why has this problem not forced itself on our attention previously? What is the struggling reader to do about the difficulty? The first question is easily answered.

It is evident that our scribe customarily wrote his letters with conscious intent to differentiate between **n** and **u**, to make his serifs join adjacent minims at the top or at the bottom appropriately. He takes pains to provide "clear links" and "clear separation". (This is one of the ways

---

1. Many modern kinds of hand-writing make these letters in comparable ways, and they include the letters **v** and **w** for good measure.

in which an expert would date the hand. Later scribes made less and less effort to be clear in this matter.) There can be no doubt about these words:

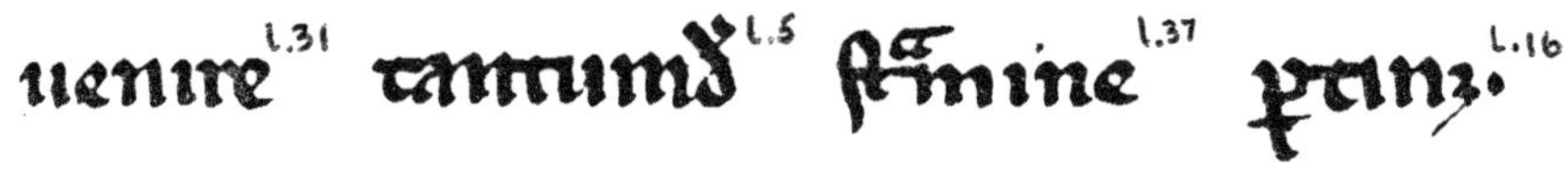

u is u and n is n . The serifs are extended in the vital place.

However, even with our scribe there are tricky moments, as we have seen. Before we return to those examples, consider this pair, which are even more rudely torn from their context than usual:

(i)  (ii) 

It is not easy to distinguish one dnu from the other dnu.

The old rules still apply: consider the meaning and the grammar of the passage, and call on your knowledge of 'common' terms. For this problem we have also one new rule, which I shall reveal shortly. But first we must establish the fuller context for each item.

(i)

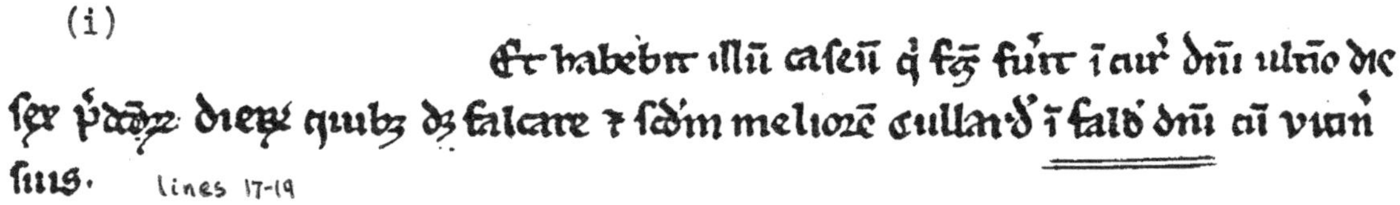

You will probably have noticed that I made the original citation of fald' dni needlessly hard by omitting the superscript line that announced, "This is a shortened word." With the fuller context that omission makes little difference. Before reading on, make your own transcript of "Et habebit...." etc. When translated, your version should include the words, "And he will have the second best ram in the lord's fold, along with his fellow-tenants" (vicinus being in this text a word for "a neighbour with the same tenure and status"). dni clearly stands for domini.

But domini will not do for the other specimen.

(ii) 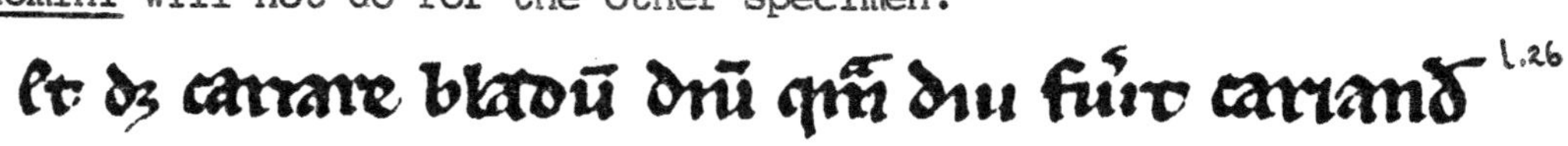

Your transcript of this should translate as "It is his duty to cart the lord's corn..........it shall be to-be-carted." What are we to make of qm dnu ? Both words are ambiguous. It seems impossible to explain dni as domini, whether genitive singular or nominative plural. qm̃ appears to be quam, but in which of its various uses? It can't mean 'than' as no comparison is being made. It can't be the relative pronoun (qui etc) as there is no feminine singular noun to be its antecedent, and no grammatical reason for an accusative in this clause. So...... we apply the new rule: COUNT THE MINIMS. This is more of a slogan than a rule. The full rule will become clear as we analyse this example.

In qm̃ dni , the tricky dni has three consecutive minims. These could in principle represent any of the following:

in ni ui iu m iii

Remembering that **u** can stand for the consonant **v**, we have to add **vi** and **iv.** The whole item could therefore be any of these:

din dni dui diu dvi div dm diii

Any of these could conceivably be a shortened word, but there is no visible mark or sign of shortening, and I have not cheated this time. Only one could be a word: diu. Ah, yes! Quam**diu** = "as long as". The scribe has written it as two words. Our Roger the Clerk has the duty to cart the lord's corn **as long as** it shall be to-be-carted - i.e. as long as there is any to cart.

The rule "Count the minims" may seem to leave us with a lot of further trial-and-error, but at the very least it serves as a check on a purely context-based guess. Any such guess should be reconsidered if it does not tally with the minim-count. The beginner should not lean too heavily on the possibility that the scribe himself may have miscounted and written one minim too few or one minim too many.

I must confess that this example is misleadingly simple. Often the number of adjacent minims is rather more than three, and the possible permutations too numerous to consider so formally. However, I have begun my discussion with such a "simple" example, because it is tempting to forget the fact that there are alternatives available and to fall for the first guess that fits. With a low minim-count this is still a sound approach. The procedure may be summarised. First study carefully the context of the tricky word. Next count the minims. Then formally set down all the possible alternatives. Eliminate the impossible and the daft. Finally decide between the survivors by reference to meaning and grammar. Again I have to remind you that what sounds tedious and clumsy soon becomes reduced to a fairly rapid and painless in-the-head proceeding.

With a greater number of minims, a compromise is called for. It is time now to consider our original examples.

(a)  .Context?  l.37
Et si grangia domini vel boveria fuerit ...pleta stramine. "And if the lord's grange or byre shall be ......with straw,...." -pleta is clearly the end of a verb made up of pleo and a prefix. There are four minims. Only one prefix in Latin consists of four minims. The word can only be **im**pleta...."filled with straw."

(b)  l.1 et sol...t de gabulo per annum vj s. The context tells us this is to do with a yearly rent of six shillings. The ending of our problem word, -t, implies a 3rd person singular verb. From our earlier assemblage of three-minim clusters, only -vi- would fit. Hence, sol**vi**t, (he pays).

(c)  l.2 This is part of the rest of the sentence just quoted. "He pays in rent per year six shillings" - 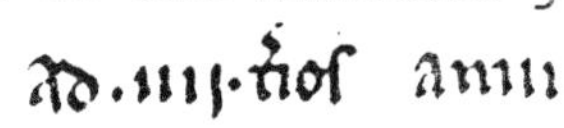 As so often one problem is adjacent to another. Let us turn for light to our "similar text" (Text IV, page 4), concerning William Avenel. There we read that he had to pay four shillings rent a year, scilicet ad quemlibet terminum xij d. So possibly tios is an abbreviated ter[m]i[n]os. Both tenants had to pay the rent on a quarterly basis (4/- divided by 4 is 12d). So the word that began this enquiry follows ad iiij terminos: "on the four term-days......." It begins with **a**. There are five minims. We are dealing with the calendar (days, quarters). One word that would fit, and it is the best we can say of it, is a**nni**, "the four term-days **of the year**".

(d)  l.37 Again we are picking up recent threads, in fact we are continuing the sentence begun in (a) above. The manuscript is as follows:
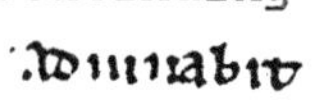 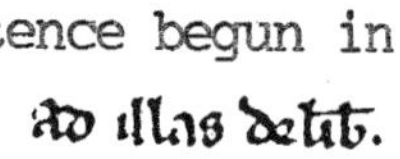 . It happens that we have already unpacked ad illas delib (see page 65) as ad illas deliberandas, which roughly must mean "to free them". As the object is not slaves or captives but buildings jammed with straw, we should perhaps say "to empty them" or "to clear them out". So what is the word on which we are focusing? We can pick out its beginning and end, **ad.....abit**. Evidently a 3rd person

singular future tense of a verb. There are again five minims. If these buildings are jammed with straw **he shall** .... to clear them out. -ven- won't do. But **-iuv-** certainly will. Not "He will come" but "He will **help**" - ad**iuv**abit.

Now try applying the procedure to the following examples:

(1.7) -  (1.33) - 

(from the Trinity College MS) - 

I have dealt at some length with minims, as they present so much difficulty in less sober hands than our scribe's. Earlier on I asked you to notice some details of the way the scribe's pen makes the strokes. I referred briefly to the 'hook' that is a mark of shortening, found particularly on **l** and **d**, suggesting that it must be a separate stroke, since in some instances it is NOT continuous with the bowl of the **d**. I hope that in the course of following this book you have noticed another fine detail. This concerns the letters **-st-**. Our scribe uses the **f**-like **s** when **t** is to follow - with what looks like a significant modification in the **t**.

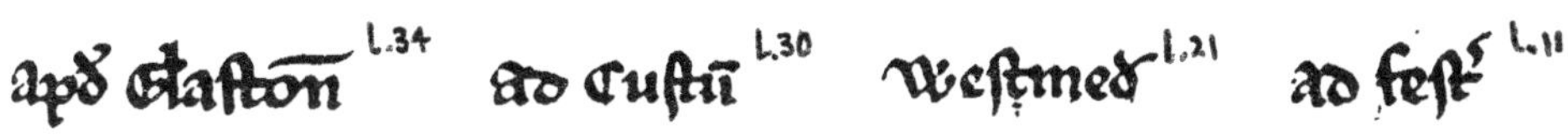

In fact, there is a movement of the pen linking the tall-**s** to the **t**. The accepted view is that this connecting mark should not be thought of as a head to the **t**. Practice with a pen may be the best way for you to investigate how this **st** was actually written. You may also like to consider whether this pairing of **t** with **s** sheds any light on the way in which the normal **c**-like **t** was written.

Talk of **c** and **t** brings us to the interpretation of  . This is a problem we have tried to dodge while concentrating on more fundamental matters. At the best of times **c** and **t** are hard to distinguish, although our scribe is more apt than many to keep them distinct. This pair of letters is definitely NOT one for fine visual discrimination. The context alone will tell you whether conventional spelling would have **-cc-** or **-tt-** or **-ct-** (or conceivably **-tc**).

It is unfortunate that each of our two instances of  has some other little problem:

(a) 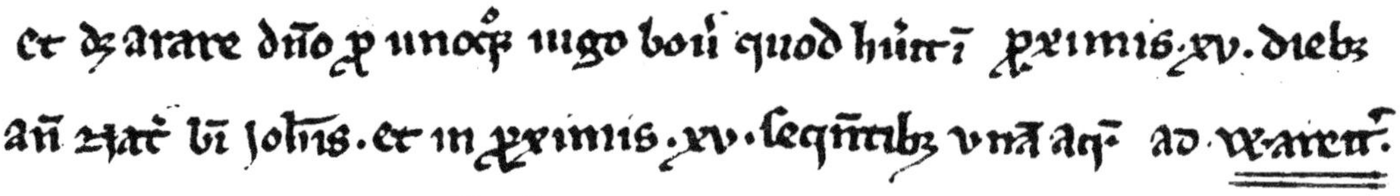 lines 3-5

(b) 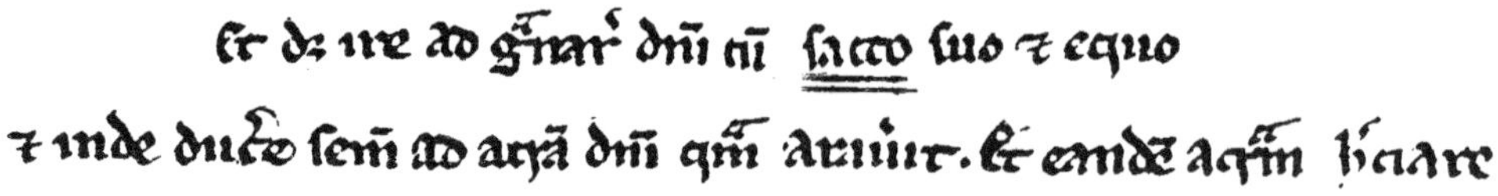 lines 6-8

(a) l.5  is the word constantly occurring in medieval Latin for "fallow". Its form is unusual, and the word is not familiar in classical Latin, although, as vervectum, it was used occasionally, e.g. by the elder Pliny. Its unusual form may account for the amazing variety of spellings recorded by Latham[1]. However, there seems little doubt that it is best to transcribe it as **warect'**.

(b) l.7 . We may well wonder what it is that Roger the Clerk has to take to the granary with his horse. The initial letter has, at least for the novice, the problem of its resemblance to **f**. If you look carefully at the undoubted **f** on line 5 in festum Sancti Martini, you will see that **f** not only has, like **s**, a little diagonal upstroke as the pen begins one main stroke; it also has an unmistakable horizontal cross-stroke, like the modern **f**. Worse is yet to come! Our scribe appears in this word actually to write identifiable **c** and **t** (unlike the seeming **tt** of warett'). Since facto is a common enough Latin word, it would be easy to read it here, - until we ask ourselves what this factum is that can be taken to the granary. Read on. Why is he going there? To fetch seed. What will he put it in? In a sack, of course. sacco. You may even wonder whether our careful scribe actually began the pair of consonants with a **c** to indicate that it is a double-**c**. That would be mere speculation. What is certain is that the context is all-important.

A variant of the problem of mis-separation of minims occurs on line 38 of the text, in a word over which I gave you over-generous help in the early stages of our study: 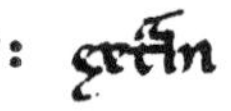. By now you will unhesitatingly read the beginning of this word as extra-, but what are we to make of the rest? There is a tall vertical, connected by the lightest thread to a strongly linked pair of minims. The natural thing would be to read this ending

1. Even the initial letter can be **g** or **b** or **v** as well as **w**.

as -ln or -lu. The Rule Of Absurdity excludes these. We are left to conclude that the links mislead. extrahi is meant.

Finally, I must draw your attention to another kind of difficulty, one that seldom arises in our text. It is a variant of the minims problem, a matter of separation, or lack of it. Just as a scribe might be careless about the division between letter and letter, so he may be unclear about the division between words.[1] He may leave a space in mid-word, or may place a word in seemingly gapless nearness to its neighbour. Presented in isolation, the rogues from our text look harmless. So once more I offer you long extracts. What comes after the Et in each case?

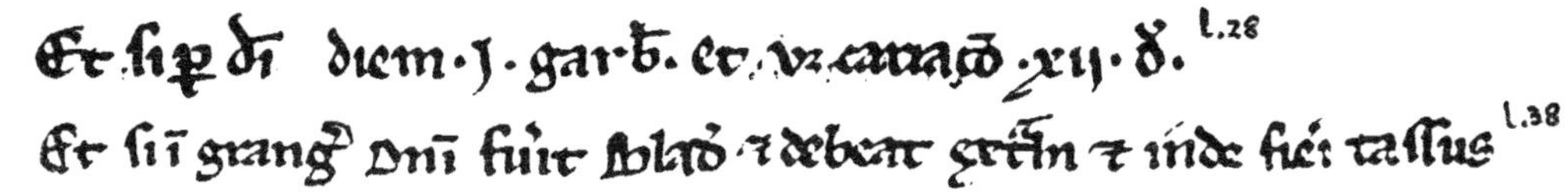

Our manifold and diverse approaches to the text have already made these sentences very familiar, so that they may present no difficulty. But you may agree that at first glance we have siper and you could possibly even read in 1.38 hi[m] or hi[n]. In fact, in each case we have two words, si per and si i[n]. Of course! If these examples seem strained, take my word for it that a useful weapon in your armoury is the knowledge that gaps may sometimes occur in the wrong places in hands more hurried than this.

By the same token you may find yourself wrestling with a more disagreeable sight, letters squashed together, usually when the scribe found that he was running out of space on his ever-precious parchment. This space-saving tendency lies at the root of the whole system of abbreviation, we may feel, especially when we notice how elaborate some of the superscript marks of 'shortening' are. It probably explains, in our text, the rather unusual super-abbreviation of domini to d' at the end of line 29.

* * * * *

A true story will serve as the epilogue to this chapter about the possibility of error arising from mis-reading of minims and spaces.

Years ago, when I first began to investigate the manorial surveys to

---

1. You will meet choice examples in a later chapter (pages 111-2).

which our text belongs, I was to be heard accosting any acquaintance who might have rural or agricultural knowledge and asking them what was the special significance of a black ox. I now realise why no helpful answer was forthcoming.

My question was based on a sentence in the survey published by the Somerset Record Society (Volume 5) as Rentalia Michaelis de Ambresbury et Rogeri de Ford[1]. It followed a familiar Glastonbury principle of making the amount of service proportionate to the resources of the tenant, according to one criterion or another. This is what the Somerset Record Society edition says:

> debet waretare domino pro unoquoque **nigro bove** quod habuerit...
> ...j acram.

It was only when a scholarly friend urged me to check the MS that I discovered the truth of the matter. The criterion was not a black ox but a yoke of oxen. Here is the manuscript version:

 = iugo boum 

The error may possibly have been not the erudite Elton's but his printer's; perhaps Elton's handwriting left something to be desired. Certainly there were clues that must have been overlooked by Elton if he himself wrote down nigro bove. Admittedly, **ni** has the same number of minims as **iu**. Admittedly, too, boū / bov̄ could be shortening of boum or bove. But the **r** was conjured out of thin air. More seriously, if the text had been bove, the relative clause following and qualifying it must have begun quem (masculine), whereas the text has quod (neuter), correctly agreeing with the neuter noun iugo. It is not sensible to ignore grammatical considerations as well as the actual letters written.

Like every story, this is capable of yielding a variety of morals. If it is possible for Homer to nod, for instance, we inferior beings need to be vigilant. More precisely, this is a case where meaning does not provide foolproof guidance. Odd it may be to use the possession of a BLACK ox as the measure of service owed, but there is not a great difference between an ox and a yoke of oxen, logically speaking. It is attention to the grammar and to the lettering that should have cast doubt on nigro bove.

---

1. ed.C.J.Elton

I trust that you have not missed the link with our text. My choice of this folio as our work-base was dictated entirely by considerations of the quality of the manuscript. It is co-incidence that it includes a sentence identical with the subect of my story, a co-incidence the more remarkable since this particular criterion for proportionate service is not common in these surveys. Both texts deal with the manor of Winterbourne (Monkton), near Avebury in Wilts. About twenty years separate the compilation of the two surveys, that published by the Somerset Record Society, and the unpublished text from which our work-material comes.

Obstinate Bits

In introducing you to the reading of medieval Latin texts through close study of a particular text I have inevitably led you towards a transcription of that text. With the help I have so far given you, your transcription must still be incomplete. This is a realistic experience for you, since on any page there are likely to be obstinate bits. It also reflects the common sense point that for many purposes a complete transcript is not necessary. I am training you to live with something less than perfection.

However, I am reluctant to discourage the enthusiastic student, and offer you now the opportunity to tackle the few remaining obstinate bits from our page. I have assembled in Text XVIII all the fragments for which you may feel you are not already prepared, together with a few quotations garnered from adjacent folios for use in the 'parallels' approach. By now you should be able to tackle these with the skills and habits you have been developing, but I propose to give you a little guidance, stage by stage. In particular, there may be some doubt here and there as to the actual problem I envisage.

The two top groups (A) are clearly to do with quolz, and I have borrowed examples from the folio following ours to make it very clear. The second group (B), from lines 3 and 10, is evidently focused on pro unoq- . huit seems also to merit attention.

The large group containing ad p'car- (C) is designed to lead you up to the final words of the longer citation, ad ut-- duos (line 29). Carefully placed under the mystery word is a repeat of the pro unoq- item, for obvious reasons. The valet items (D) put three small coins together.

I have again borrowed examples to help with p'dco- (E), and provided the context from which our own example comes (lines 17-18). The long quotation from line 23 (F) is simply to provide the context for metend'; line 26 provides a parallel. In lines 15-16 (G) the crucial word is tm̄. This job lot ends (H) with herciat' (lines 8-9) and tot- (line 16).

Before turning to page 86 for further help, see what you can do unaided.

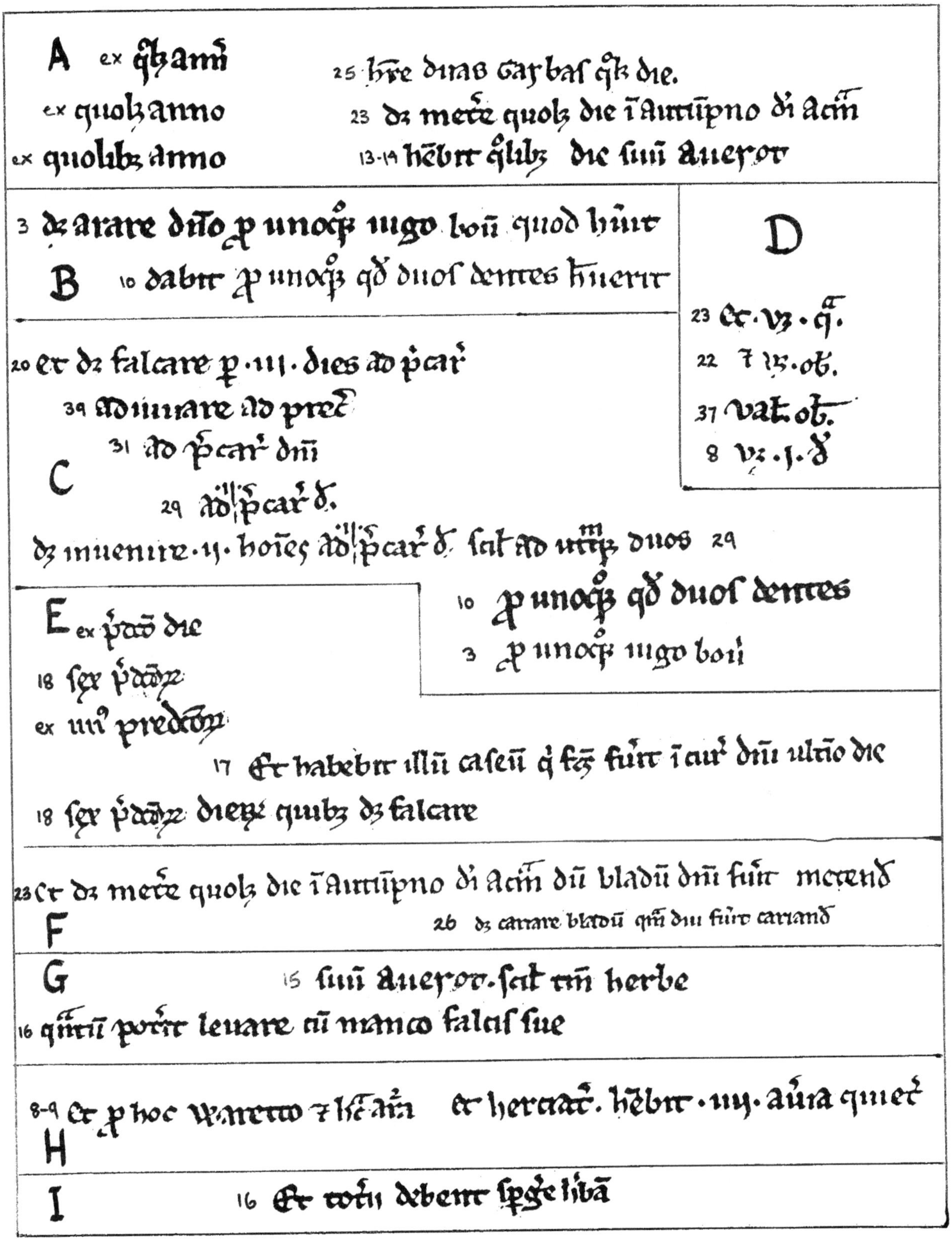

Text XVIII

Numbers refer to lines of the standard text (page 7 etc).
ex indicates a borrowing from other folios of the MS.

A. The first group in Text XVIII reminds you that there are two ways of writing quo, and more importantly that ʒ can mean either -et simply, or a chunk that ends -et. Here the chunk is -ibet.

B. With unoq-, ʒ is clearly NOT -ibet or even -et. To cut a long story short, turn back to page 46. From this we deduce the rather overdue lesson that final ʒ can mean **-que** in addition to -et and -bus. As for huit, I generously transcribed this member of the habeo family on page 66. In a later chapter I shall be advising you to be on the look-out for this particular tense, unmistakable in the second example of the pair, ... duos dentes h**uerit**.

C. The standard Latin expression for boonwork appears in ad p'car- . I revealed on page 51 that it can be singular or plural. The ambiguity of "two men for two boonworks" (total of 4 man-days or 2?) is sorted out by ad ut- duos, "two for each". The classical Latin for "each [of two]" is, of course, uterque. (Now you see why I repeated unoquoque beneath it.) Here it is accusative after ad, and feminine to agree with the implied precariam. Between the ut- and the -que the only help we have is a superscript **m**. But then that is usual with superscript letters (see p.57 and Key) - to indicate a prominent letter from an omitted group of letters. Your knowledge of the declension of uterque has to fill in the rest.

D. Denarius and obolus you should know by now. Quadrans for a farthing may be unfamiliar, and not easy to guess from q .

E. The sentence from lines 17-18 refers back to lines 12-13: debet falcare pratum domini per vj dies. We have previously tackled most of lines 17-18, albeit piecemeal. (See, for instance, pages 63 and 66.) You ought before turning to this page of help to have got as far as this: Et habebit illum caseum qui factus fuerit in curia domini ultimo die.... I suggest you now refer back to the paragraphs on page 48, about the composite letter+sign so often used for genitives plural.[1] So we have the last day "**of** the six ... days on which he has to mow." They are days of which the writer has already spoken, "aforesaid". The borrowed examples now serve their purpose. The pre- equals "afore-". We have just expanded fcs to factus; most likely -dco is -dicto (equals "-said"). predictorum dierum , in fact.

1. Note that the **r** in the suspended dierum is in fact a CAPITAL **R**.

We have already met part of the extract from lines 23-4 (see the top of Text XVIII), and the remainder is closely paralleled by the little quotation from line 26. *metend'* is easily recognised as a gerundive. The snag is the harmless looking *dū*. In fact it IS harmless, the superscript line being Old Faithful himself, the sign of omitted **m** or **n**.

tm̄ looks very innocent, too. If you consider it, however, you will realise that it is a contraction, and there are many possibilities (*tam*, *tum*, *tamen* etc.) As always, look at the context. "He shall have every day his *averoc* [whatever that may be, - but wait, he explains!], that is to say, ... of hay .... he can lift with the handle of his scythe." The text goes on to say what happens if greed causes the man to overload the tool. I expect you remember now the discussion on page 64, where I actually supplied a translation. So *tm̄ herbe quantum* [ll.15-16] means "as much hay as...". The correlative to *quantum* is *tant***um**. Q.E.D.

Et pro hoc warecto et hac arura et, [l.9] you should be reading by now. So the completion of *herciat'* is likely to make it ablative singular of a noun, parallel to *warecto* and *arura*. The stem is obvious, *herci-* meaning 'harrow'. Latham supplies the noun, *herciat***ura**, which will also be the written form of the ablative.

It is difficult to resist transcribing the final sample as *Et totum debent spargere herbam*. [l.16] To do so, we must disregard the distinctly eccentric use of the twist above the MIDDLE letter as a sign of the missing FINAL **m**. We must also disregard the lack of agreement between *totum* and *herbam*. This challenge is dangerous. Remember the "black ox" (page 82)?

Effort is rewarded. You are now, I hope, in a position to make a complete transcription of the full page from which I have taken so much illustrative material. Text XIX is a copy of the complete page. As you have already wrestled with the first thirteen lines, they are now in reduced type, but I have spaced out the remaining lines to make them clearer. Remember the rules: make your transcript on a numbered line-by-line basis; use a pencil, at least for any material over which you have the slightest doubt; when in doubt, refer first to the rest of the page of the MS, certainly not to books of reference. Of course you may wish to refresh your memory by reference to notes you have made or to the points discussed in this book. But essentially, the MS text is your reference-book. Do the easy bits first, but beware of jumping to conclusions. As you build up a full version, your grasp of the meaning will improve, and this may modify your view of the context surrounding a difficult word. On no account turn to the version in Appendix D for help until you are satisfied you have left no stone unturned. Resist the temptation to check up bit by bit, at all costs. That would reduce disastrously the benefit of the exercise.

Rog's clicus ten' .i. virgat' tre 7 soluit de Gablo p annu .vi. s. .d. .iii. nos
annu. et de dono ad Hidar' .xi. d. et d3 lauare 7 tonde oues dni cu alijs
vicinis suis. 7 v3 hoc .ii. d. et de arare dno p unoqq iugo boū quod hui't i
primis .xv. dieb3 añ ... Sci Johis. et in primis .xv. sequentib3 vna acr'
ad Warett'. Et tantumd' d3 arare dno i q'nden p'x añ fest sci Martini. 7 i
q'nden p'x sequen. et v3 arura .iiii. boū .xiiii. d. Et d3 ire ad ... dni cu
sacco suo 7 equo 7 inde duce sem' ad acra dni qm aruit. Et eande acra
herciare 7 v3 .i. d. Et dns inueniet seminatore. Et p hoc Waretto 7 lib'a .
et herciat'. hebit .iiii. a'ıa cu bob3 dni. i pastur' quiet de herbag' si
p'a a'ıa hunt qm .iiii. dabit p unoqq qd duos dentes hu'erit .ii. den.
ad Gula Augusti. et ad fest sci Andr' .iii. d. Et p quol3 q dente no huit
.i. d. ad Gulam Augusti. Et ad fest sci Andr' .i. d. ob. Et d3 falcare p'tum
dni p .vi. dies de ... in Suthmede. et val3 .vi. d. Et hebit q'lib3
die unu auerot. scit tm herbe qntu poterit leuare cu manico falcis sue
sicut ptin3 ad auerot 7 manic' no tang3 t'ram. 7 si manic' i illa h'ba leua
d' frangatur: p'd3 h'bam 7 nulla alia mia ptin3. Et totu debent sp'ge h'ba
7 ferre acra ad falc' acuend. Et habebit illu caseu q f'c9 fuit i cur' dni ultio die
sex p'd'cor dier' quib3 d3 falcare 7 scdm meliore cullard' i fald' dni cu vicin
suis. Et si dns nullu Cullard' nl' multon' i fald' sua heret. hebit p'do die
p ipo Cullardo cu Vicinis suis .xii. d. Et d3 falcare p .iii. dies ad p'car' i
Westmed'. 7 n' h'bit .7 v3 .vi. d. et d3 leuare p'tu 7 v3 .v. d. 7 cariare fenu.
Et v3 .iii. d. Et fac' mullon 7 v3 .ob. Et d3 sercelare cu .i. hoie p' nona. p .i.
diem. et v3 .q'. Et d3 mete' quol3 die i Autupno di acra du bladu dni fuit
metend' prec' diem sabbi 7 hēre una garbam p corigia. Et v3 messio .x. d.
Et p duos dies i Autupno una acra integra 7 hre duas garbas q'l3 die.
7 v3 messio .ii. d. Et d3 cariare bladu dni qm diu fuit cariand. 7 qndo ca
riat no deb3 mete'. et qn metit no d3 cariare. Et qn cariat tota die he
bit duas garbas sep' meliores i ultima caretta qm cariauit. Et si p di
diem .i. garb. et v3 cariacio .xii. d. Et d3 inuenire .ii. hoies ad p'car' d.
i Autupno. scit ad uniqq duos 7 debent bis comede ad Custu dni i pan. cer
uis 7 companag. 7 v3 messio .iiii. d. Et d3 uenire ad p'car' dni cu caru
ca sua de consuetudie semel i anno. ad ...magiu 7 herciare cu equo suo qn
tum arat. Et dns pasc3 illu 7 herciatorem suu semel in die i pan. c'uis et
companag. Et d3 summagiare t' in Anno apd Glaston. scit qual3 vice di
qr. Et q'l3 vice h're de dono dni cu vicinis suis .ii. d. scit ipe et omis q
summagiant. Et v3 summagiacio .xviii. d. Et si grangia dni vl' bou'ia fu
erit impleta f'mine: adiuuabit cu .i. hoie ad illas delib'. Et val. ob.
Et si i grang' dni fuit bladu 7 debeat c'rib'n 7 inde fiei tassus. deb3 cu .i.
hoie adiuuare ad prec' 7 no de consuetudie. Et d3 cariare corrediu dni

Text XIX

Punctuation

There is reason to believe[1] that in the Middle Ages it was generally the custom to read aloud, not silently. For such a practice, punctuation served a purpose very different from the punctuation of modern text. Punctuation marks were primarily used as indicators of suitable places for a pause, and in more sophisticated types of writing there was choice of marks according to the length of pause thought desirable or necessary. Equally foreign to our practice is the common habit of separating numerals from text on either side by a point or dot: primis.xv.dieb; . It is remarkable how prevalent is the belief that the punctuation of modern texts, which are designed to be read silently, skimmed, or scanned, is in fact a series of pause-marks. No doubt a person who in fact reads such a text aloud will have pauses as one of the considerable array of devices by which to express the meaning of the text. But the system of punctuation that has evolved is largely related to the logic of the material and also to its grammar.

From this divergence of practice arises a nettle that the transcriber must grasp. Faithfulness is always regarded as a cardinal virtue in one who transcribes another's text. But modern readers are not familiar with the medieval system. It seems that you must therefore either preserve the medieval punctuation, such as it is, and leave readers to make what they can of it, or abandon the punctuation of the manuscript text, and punctuate along modern lines. In any case it would be pointless to reproduce the dots that some scribes put after every abbreviated word, not to mention those that seem "to be no more than evidence of the place at which a scribe rested his pen..."[2]. Study of published texts will reveal compromises that some scholars have adopted.

Related to this is the syntax of medieval Latin. In many texts, this was fully as complex as in classical Latin, but the kind of administrative material often encountered by historical students makes less use of the more complicated structures (i.e.of subordinate clauses and participial phrases). These occur mainly when a simple statement is qualified in some way. In our

---

1. See M.T.Clanchy, From Memory To Written Record.

2. L.C.Hector op.cit. His discussion of punctuation will be invaluable when you have more experience.

text the various occurrences of *quando* and *si* illustrate the point. e.g.

pro hoc... habebit iiij averia quieta de herbagio. Et si plura averia habuerit quam iiij, dabit........

In our text and numerous others, comparable items of information are set down one after another, linked usually by the simple *et*, though in some texts the more formal *Item* is found.[1] From this practice the modern use of the expression "an item" derives.

The consequence is a text, as you will have noticed, where the full stop (as we would say) followed by *et* is the single, universal, device for both separating items of information and suggesting continuity.

In my chapter on capital letters I left on one side the question of their use. If the modern notion of a sentence is inappropriate in a text like this, it is not entirely surprising that there was no uniformity about beginning a 'sentence' with a capital letter. The matter is complicated by the fact that medieval scribes made free use of shortened signs for *et*, commonly ⁊ . However, our scribe was often happy to write this word in full. Against this virtue must be set his indifference about the size of an initial **e** when it did not take the form of the distinctive capital **E***. Some instances are so large that we must suppose they are equivalent to a capital. Unfortunately, we can find every graduation in size:

The upshot of all this is clear: a reader of this particular text, at least, must disregard the capital and pseudo-capital letter **E** of Et. What to do about the long series of 'sentences' beginning with *Et* is a matter of taste Whether you place a full-stop or a comma, or no stop at all, before such an *Et*, the result is unlikely to feel comfortable to the modern eye.

---

1. From elsewhere in our MS we have this mixture of *et*, ⁊ , and *Item* abbreviated.

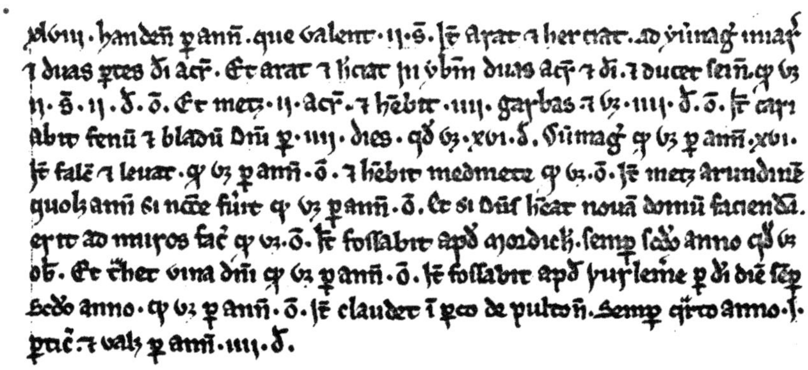

(See Key)

Not Strictly Classical

Medieval Latin is a useful term insofar as it refers to Latin written some time after the collapse of Rome and before modern times. It would be wrong to think it implies some kind of uniformity about that Latin, since classical Latin also was of many kinds. However, some features of texts such as the one we have been studying may take unawares the student whose last experience of Latin was with Caesar and Ovid. This chapter explains some of the more general features of medieval Latin that may be strange to you, but in any event you need to bear in mind my advice about looking at "material similar in kind" before you start work on a new text.(See page 3.)

SPELLING

Despite the prevalence of the methods of shortening to which I have devoted so much space, it can be safely stated that the Latin of the period (unlike most of the vernacular[1] texts of that time) was generally spelt with consistency[2]. Where a spelling variant occurs regularly, we should consider the possibility that pronunciation may have changed also. Scribes followed NON-classical conventions in the following respects:

(a) **e** was regularly used instead of classical **ae**.

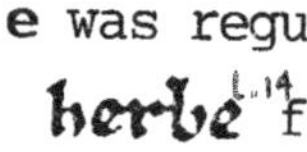 for herbae and  for falcis suae

(b) The classical modification of **m** to **n** before **d** was by no means strictly maintained. For eandem and tantundem we have

 but 

(c) **h** at the beginning of a word was a problem then as now, e.g. **h**arare for arare (to plough). In our present text we have yvernagium for **h**yvernagium (see next items).

(d) **i** could be replaced by **y**. e.g. 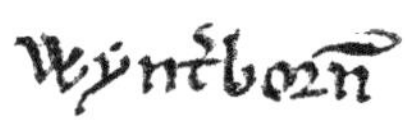 Wynterborn'

(e) **b** could become **v** (as in gu**v**erno for gu**b**erno, to steer or govern). Hence **hib**ernagium is 

---

1. I use the term to stand for the various 'native' languages in contrast to the universality of Latin.

2. It follows that English place-names and technical terms occurring in our texts are NOT spelt consistently. In our source occurs a term foruhtha. Latham cites this and also forerda, forherda, forhurtha, forurda.

(f) We need to remember that our school classics texts used a conventionalised spelling, and that in all periods **v** and **u** were interchangeable as signs to represent both the vowel and the consonant sounds: **uno vnā ut vt**

(g) Less generalised changes occurred, like the preference for -ch- in michi and nichil for mihi and nihil.

(h) There was some looseness in the matter of double letters, e.g. atentus for attentus occurs.

(i) Some scribes compressed words or ran two together, as premineo (=pre-emineo) and imperpetuum (=in perpetuum).

GRAMMAR

In both the changes within words (Accidence) and the rules governing these changes (Syntax), the Latin of medieval texts is best seen as selection from the apparatus of classical Latin.

ACCIDENCE. There are very few deviations to be found from classical word-endings. Perhaps the most regular is the assimilation of vetus and of all comparative adjectives to the regular third declension ablative singular ending. You will remember that whereas the main third declension adjectives in classical Latin have ablative singular in -**i**, (acri, ingenti, gravi), vetus and the comparatives end that case in -**e** (vetere, meliore). In medieval texts you are likely to find veteri, meliori etc. in the ablative singular. An apparent deviation, declining Greek names in the Greek form, was normal in classical times. Thus we have Andreas (Andrew) with the Greek genitive Andree(Andreae in classical Latin), and we find regularly the Greek accusative of Pentecostes, i.e. Pentecosten.

As for verbs, you may not often encounter the full range of subjunctives, but there are no important novelties to fear.

SYNTAX. I have already mentioned syntax (pages 90-91). Our standard text has no noun clauses, plentiful quite orthodox adjectival clauses, and a sprinkling of the simpler kinds of adverbial clauses, i.e. those with the indicative mood of the verb. On the other hand, you will meet subjunctives in main clauses regularly, especially in the "Be it known..." preamble to charters. This is commonly expressed by the perfect subjunctive, Noveritis, a form that cannot be translated literally into English. It is, of course, good classical Latin.

However, although our scribe may not need to wrestle with the subtleties of hypothetical conditionals, he is au fait with the use of the future-perfect tense in ordinary factual conditional and temporal clauses (e.g. fuerit in lines 36-37). Always be on the look-out for this tense.

There was one matter where medieval usage had developed a rule additional to the classical rule. In classical Latin reported statements were expressed by the "accusative and infinitive" construction. In medieval texts this construction still occurs, but we also find quod followed by the indicative, exactly like "He said **that** .....", "Il a dit **que**...." in modern languages.

Much less significant are the various points at which a medieval writer prefers to use a preposition where classical writers do not (such as cum used instrumentally on line 14), or where medieval writers prefer a preposition other than the one that is familiar in classical Latin, such as super to mean "on" or "at".

VOCABULARY

It is hardly surprising that in medieval texts we find words and usages unknown to classical writers. Several classes of words deserve comment.

1. Words known in classical times but now used with a new meaning:

gula (throat) was used in C.L. metaphorically for "appetite", and now becomes "opening", of a water-course, or of a month.

misericordia we have already mentioned. From being the lord's "mercy" on which you threw yourself it became the "mercy" which he allowed you, i.e. the penalty he inflicted on you.

quilibet changes dramatically from "any" to "every".

vicinus, as we have seen, could mean "of the same tenure" as well as geographically "neighbouring".

2. Words not found in classical Latin but manifestly formed from classical Latin words:

From *hibernus* (wintry) we have *hibernagium* (winter sowing).

From *lardum* (bacon) we have *lardarium* (larder) - in this text a kind of tax, money for the abbot's larder.

From *quindeni* (fifteen each) we have *quindena* (fortnight).

From *virga* (rod or stick) we have *virgata* (yard-land).

3. Words not recorded in classical times - and often the core vocabulary of administrative documents. I have listed in Appendix C the chief words of this kind from our text, so I will just provide four examples here:

4. Words that do not even pretend to be Latin:

(lines 14,15)

(from another source)

Why Bother?

Students who toiled earnestly through my chapters on the scribal signs of abbreviation might be forgiven if they wondered at times if the signs were really necessary. To reflect at all on the various ways in which language can be written down is to increase this doubt. Let us consider the matter seriously.

Study for a moment the advertisements copied here. Shortened words abound: Spac. det. dble. Gd.

If the comparison interests you, see if you can make some sort of classification of the various shortenings.

Certainly you will be inclined to agree that the omission of letters has not drastically impaired understanding of the text.

But it must be admitted that the words shortened comprise a limited group, and the experienced house-seeker knows them by heart.

POOLE. Spac. det. BUNGALOW. 3 dble. bedrm. 1 en-suite. 4 yr. N.H.B.C. remaining. Dble. garage, boat space. Gd. gdn. Adjacent all amenities. £120,000 o.n.o. Ph.: (0202) 687225. [0874–23PA

POOLE, Broadstone. Secluded, immac., fully modernised first floor flat. Block of 4. F/hold. 2 dble. bedrms., large balcony overlkg. copse. Garage. Walking distance shops. £88,000. No chain. Ph.: (0452) 20243. [0589–24PA

POOLE, Parkstone. Det. 2 bedrm. HOUSE, det. garage, parking. Quiet cul-de-sac, close amenities. New kit., sun lounge, ,feature archway, bathrm./shower, sep. toilet. Secluded gdn. Workshop, greenhse., chalet. No chain. Offers £70,000. Ph.: (0202) 738457. [0669–25PA

POOLE. 3 bedrmd. det. HOUSE, gas c/h. Parking for 3 cars. 4 miles Bournemouth. Gd. decor. £99,950. Ph.: (0202) 742794. [0811–25PA

SWANAGE. Second floor flat. 200 yards beach. Lounge, diner, dble. bedrm., shower rm. Car space. Ideal first time buyer. Holiday home or retirement. £47,000.. Ph.: (0929) 423266. [0873–32PA

WIMBORNE. Ground floor 2 bedrm. flat with garage. Overlkg. Wimborne. Minster & gdns. 95 yr. lease. £92,000. Ph.: (0202) 841815. [0916–23PA

DEVON, Torquay. Nice family home. 3/4 bedrms. Gas c/h., new roof. Gdns. No chain. Gd. cond. £60,000. Ph.: (0803) 528753 after 3 p.m. [0729–22PA

DEVON, Ashburton. Mod. det. BUNGALOW, 2 bedrms. C/h. Landscaped gdn. Lovely views. Will accept £75,000 for immediate sale. Ph.: (0364) 52529 or 081 994 3185. [0791–25PA

HONITON. 3 bedrm. mod. f/hold. semi BUNGALOW, c/h., dble. glaz. Secluded gdn., patio, garage. No chain. £72,000. Ph.: Honiton 41573. [0548–24PA

For writers needing to get language down on paper at high speed, various forms of short-hand have been devised. One of the earliest was devised by Cicero's freedman-secretary, Tiro, whose name still serves as the label for the form of "and"(⁊) that he used. A fairly late entrant into the field was the Hills' <u>Teeline</u> (1968), which is not actually called "short-hand" but "fast writing". Its two main principles are eliminating unnecessary letters and reducing the movement needed to form the remaining letters. This, of course, is not selective like House-Agents-ese, but applied to every word. Here is a sample of the description of their alphabet .

H — Only the downstroke is written and this rests on the line.

J — Written as a single downstroke, through the line, *without loop or dot.*

K (ck) — The straight downstroke is omitted, leaving only the angle. Like c this character may be used to represent the combination ck

L — (or) This is a single stroke, boldly curved. It is generally written downward but may be turned upwards for convenience or to avoid writing too far below the writing line.

M — The initial hook and middle stem of the ordinary written m are omitted, leaving a single wide arch written from left to right with one stroke.

Teeline also uses what it calls "contractions" or "single character abbreviations":

auto

be

do, department

electric, error

page, pence

quantity, queen

railway

southern

For wholeheartedness in reduction to the bare essentials, however, there is no rival to Hebrew. Look first at this sample of Hebrew in its fullest printed form, taken from the Old Testament. You will perhaps guess that the main characters are in fact consonants and the tiny dots and lines represent vowels.

א וַיְהִי כְּכַלּוֹת שְׁלֹמֹה לִבְנוֹת אֶת־בֵּית יְהוָה וְאֶת־בֵּית הַמֶּלֶךְ
וְאֵת כָּל־חֵשֶׁק שְׁלֹמֹה אֲשֶׁר חָפֵץ לַעֲשׂוֹת׃ וַיֵּרָא 2
יְהוָה אֶל־שְׁלֹמֹה שֵׁנִית כַּאֲשֶׁר נִרְאָה אֵלָיו בְּגִבְעוֹן׃
3 וַיֹּאמֶר יְהוָה אֵלָיו שָׁמַעְתִּי אֶת־תְּפִלָּתְךָ וְאֶת־תְּחִנָּתְךָ
אֲשֶׁר הִתְחַנַּנְתָּה לְפָנַי הִקְדַּשְׁתִּי אֶת־הַבַּיִת הַזֶּה אֲשֶׁר
בָּנִתָה לָשׂוּם שְׁמִי־שָׁם עַד־עוֹלָם וְהָיוּ עֵינַי וְלִבִּי שָׁם כָּל־

Compare the text on this page with that printed on the previous page. This is an 'unpointed' version of the other, i.e. it lacks the vowel 'pointing'.[1]

1. ויהי ככלות שלמה לבנות את־בית יהוה ואת־
בית המלך ואת כל־חשק שלמה אשר חפץ לעשות:
2. וירא יהוה אל־שלמה ויאמר אליו שמעתי את־
תפלתך ואת־תחנתך אשר התחננתה לפני הקדשתי
את־הבית הזה אשר בנתה לשום שמי־שם עד־
עולם והיו עיני ולבי שם כל־הימים: 3. ואתה אם

Alarming as it may seem, not only is it possible to learn to read unpointed Hebrew, but in fact historically it came first. The vowel points were introduced later.

It is difficult to resist the conclusion that one might perfectly well read medieval Latin script without paying any attention at all to the various marks or signs added to the reduced forms of words. Let us test the hypothesis. What do you make of this?

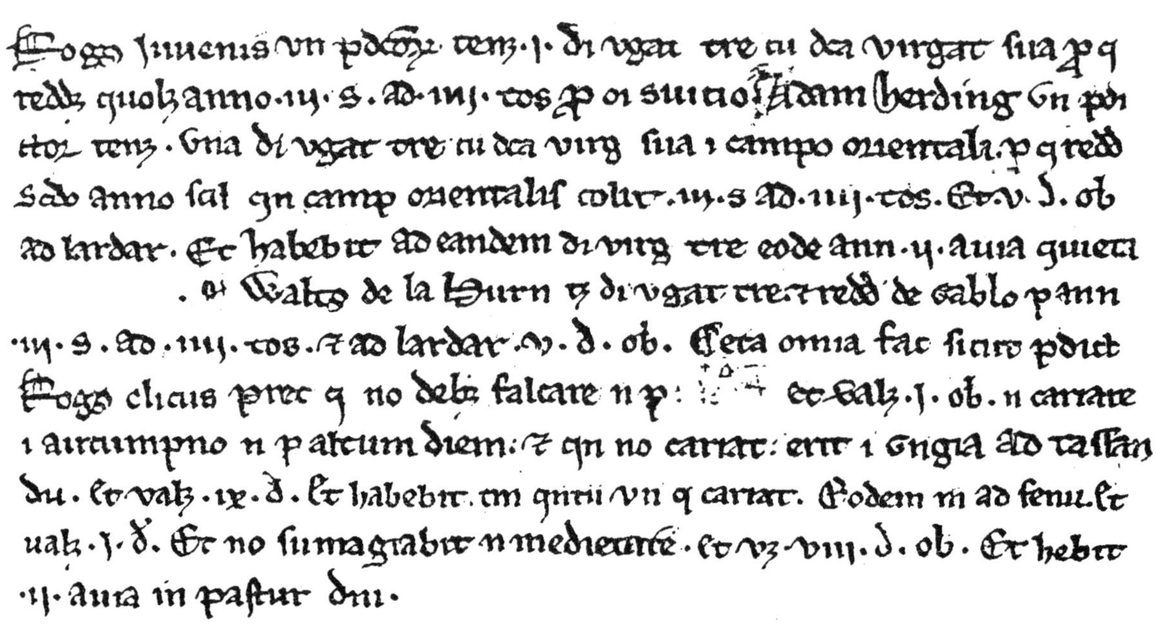
Rogs Juuenis un pdict tenz .j. di vgat tre cu dca virgat sua p q
redd quolz anno .iij. s. ad .iiij. tos p oi suitio. Adam herding un pdi
ctoz tenz. Gna di vgat tre cu dca virg sua i campo orientali. p q redd
sdo anno sal qn camp orientalis colit .iij. s ad .iiij. tos. Et .v. d. ob
ad lardar. Et habebit ad eandem di virg tre eode ann .ij. aura quieta
. oi Walto de la Burn q di vgat tre. 7 redd de sablo p ann
.iij. s. ad .iiij. tos. 7 ad lardar .v. d. ob. Cetera omia fac sicut pdict
Rogs clicus ptet q no deb falcare n p: [illegible] et val .j. ob. n carrare
i autumpno n p altum diem: 7 qn no carrat: erit i Sngia ad tassan
du. et val .ix. d. Et habebit tm qntu un q carrat. Eodem m ad fenu. Et
ualz .j. d. Et no sumagiabit n medietate. et vz .viij. d. ob. Et hebit
.ij. aura in pastur dni.

1. As a matter of fact, it also lacks a few complete words contained in the pointed version.

Even at your relatively early stage in palaeography you probably managed to decipher a fair amount of the text. You will find an undoctored copy of the text in the Key, to enable you to check your version.

What conclusion follows from the experiment? In my view there are several points to set against the superficial impression you may have formed that the signs of shortening are unnecessary.

First there is the inescapable fact that the smaller the evidence you draw on, the greater the chance of error.. In my saga of the black ox it was clear that the transcriber did not bring the full available evidence to bear on the decipherment of the apparently tricky word. The neuter relative pronoun quod should have excluded the possibility of a masculine antecedent, causing the reader to re-think his interpretation of the minims. The matter is of greater weight when the written short-word is capable of various expansions and the scribal signs give some indication of the probable omission. A simple **p** could have a number of meanings. The provision of a superscript **t** at least reduces the field, suggesting post or potest. To ignore the **t** leaves open possibilities like per, pius, presens, publicus, persona.........

Through sheer carelessness I once read

as infra la **Sinu**dich, ignoring the superscript 'twist' which might have led me to the correct reading **Sumer**dich. This, of course, is a place-name, and therefore far less predictable than a common noun. But then proper nouns are very much a feature of historical text, and already made difficult by the uncertainties of capital letters. With them, certainly, we need every shred of information the scribe provides.

Another point to consider is the mere fact that the system of providing the marks of shortening lasted so long. It is true that the human mind can continue to be mistaken about matters of fact for long periods, and it may be that, contrary to belief, marks of shortening were actually unnecessary. However, it is difficult to reject the presumption that medieval scribes themselves thought the marks to be useful.

Looking beyond medieval Latin, it said by students of linguistics that language (unlike Maths) tends to favour redundancy. That is to say, in all aspects of language (speech, writing, grammar, etc) there are often more clues employed than are absolutely necessary. Presumably this tendency helps to safeguard meaning against the contrary tendency of human beings to cut corners and so make mistakes. Thus in English the use of a distinctive pronoun like 'he' would be sufficient; there is no actual need for a distinctive verb ending as well ('has' as opposed to 'have', 'thinks' as opposed to 'think')[1]. So we would be wise not to ignore 'unnecessary' clues.

My own conclusion would be that, if you are prudent, you will gain as thorough a mastery as possible of the system, such as it was. Experience will eventually bring its own balance of skimming and scrutiny. Mistrust those who profess to despise a concern for detail. High-speed readers of modern printed text forget the stages by which they first mastered our complex systems of spelling and printing.

May I offer you as a post-script a further observation based on the study of children learning to read? Mistakes are not matters for regret. From them we can learn, especially if we are able to see the nature of the mistake, and remember it. You will have noticed that I myself act on this principle, and have tried to smooth your path by examples of my own errors.

---

1. In fact, of course, in many cases the distinctive form has disappeared ("I thought", "he thought", "I had", "he had").

Another Hand, Another text

Long before this you should have been asking, "This is all very well, but how successfully shall I apply this knowledge to other scribal hands?" In this chapter I offer you text of a different nature, written in a different hand. To be kind, I have not gone to extremes of unlikeness.

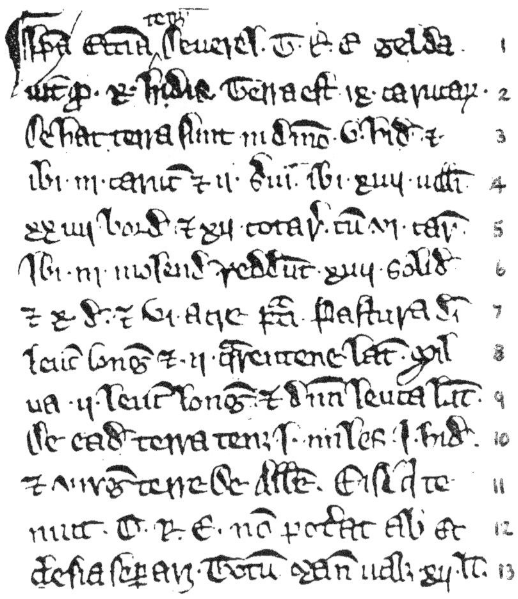

Text XX

It is important that at this stage you practise the skills and habits you have built up. Applying these, you will manage many of the more straightforward parts, and this success will give you confidence when you come to "obstinate bits".

Your first step is, as before, to work from unambiguous whole words. Copy, in the most careful imitation of the original that you can manage, all the whole words that you can spot. I will give you one warning, however. This scribe did not always provide clear marks of shortening, so the lack of such marks is no sure sign of a whole word. Instead you must confine your search to whole words that you can recognise.

Next, build up this scribe's alphabet. You may feel, as you scrutinise the whole words, that this hand is not, after all, so very different from the hand responsible for our standard text. That is true. But the strokes in some letters definitely are new, and some new features are shared by several letters. At least make sure you have identified the most obvious of these. You will notice that there are several capitals, some at least being exactly what we have met before. Check that there are no new confusibles. Are **c** and **t** easily distinguishable? What about the letters for which we have learnt two separate forms......?

At this first stage I don't want to spoon-feed you, so my observations on the scribe's letter-forms are placed in Appendix E. If possible, go on to the next step without comparing your findings with mine. Go through the text again, seeing what part-words you can now transcribe. Look out for the more helpful signs of shortening you have learnt, always mindful that individual scribes had their own preferences and whims.

Now that you have had a thorough look at the new scribal hand, unaided, I shall not be giving too much away if I list some of the general points that should emerge as you identify some part-words. You will find fuller detail again in Appendix E

Familiar faces appear: 
as well as both uses of , one in the acres of "meadow" and the other in a word not encountered in our study so far, quarentene (furlongs). There are also instances of the superscript line to indicate omitted **m** or **n**. Harder to spot is the superscript letter **i** above a **q** to make qui. You could also be forgiven for not recognising two **er** signs : the mark above **s** in the middle of line 4 (itself a tricky letter to make out) and above the first **t** in potat in line 12.

That several words are suspended is obvious from their non-Latin endings. Some have no mark to say that the ending has been cut short, like molend (line 6); that is, if we can trust the rather faint reproduction of the text. The rest seem mainly to be adorned with a sign we have not studied before, rather like a horizontal bracket (as on caruc in line 4). It can be regarded as a curved version of the superscript line. It also serves as a sign of contraction, as in ecclesia on line 1.

Have you recognised the text? The give-away clue is on line 1, with the unmistakable word-stem Gelda-, and, as you probably know, this form of tax was a feature of the Domesday record. If you are at all familiar with transcriptions or translations of your local Domesday entries you may be a little better equipped to decipher this text. (N.B. This text is a later copy, not the original Domesday text!) Remember my advice on preparing your mind by reading published text of a similar kind (page 3). You will at least expect reference to various classes of peasant, and to ploughs and mills.

What new hazards has this text for you? You may already have noticed a fair sprinkling of words split in half by the ending of a line, but with no apparent warning, whereas our principal study-text was occasionally graced at such a point by the provision of a faint diagonal line(e.g. at the end of line 32 of that text). This is particularly misleading on line 12 of our present text, where there appears to be a bold Et. Careful study of the first 'word' on line 13 should yield "clesia". Armed with my warning you will combine the two to give Ecclesia.

The last 'word' on line 8 has a most obscure first letter, but the final -il is clear enough, as is the -ua at the beginning of line 9. Adopting the crossword-puzzler's method, "blank-**i-l-u-a**" (or, of course, ...-**v-a**) leaves you little choice but silva. The words split at the end of lines 1 and 11 should present no problems.

You will have noticed the tiny word above line 1. It seems that a word had been left out, the omission noticed, and rectified in a way we ourselves would use. In other texts you may find the inserted word or letters in the margin. I think that the fourth of these tiny letters is meant to be the ʒ for -et. A problem you will have to face when making formal transcriptions is how best to deal with insertions, deletions and other alterations to the text. In a heavily up-dated text a major issue is where to print the changes that the scribe has squeezed into tiny spaces.

Finally, we have an example of one of the standard signs being used in one of its exceptional meanings. You have learnt that **p** with a line through its descender normally means per. It is easy to forget the word "normally". Taking the sign in its normal sense, we would have in line 13 seperari. Manifestly it here means -par- to give us separari. I shall return to this in my next chapter.

I have already reminded you that a new text offers not only new problems but new opportunities to apply your battery of skills and habits . One of the practices that seems to me fundamental is the discovery and exploitation of parallels. This text affords a useful example of how parallel passages contribute to the resolving of doubtful suspensions. Towards the end of 1.7 a passage begins which should not be too difficult to transcribe as a set of part-words:

Pastura di- leuc- long-

Also, Silva ij leuc- long- (line 9).

As leuca means a "league" (a measure of distance) we may surmise that we have here the dimensions of pasture and woodland, and that di- is dimidi- (half).

The first obvious step would seem to be to complete long- . "The pasture is ....long." "The woodland is ...... long." Or so it seems. So cautiously one suggests longa for both clauses. It remains to be seen if this is right.

Next, what will be the appropriate endings to leuc- in each clause, bearing in mind that the first will be singular (because a half-league) and the second plural (because two leagues)?

In classical Latin the accusative would be found, and therefore, lacking contrary evidence, one should complete the suspended words appropriately:

Pastura dimidiam leucam longa

Silva ij leucas longa

Unfortunately there are four phrases of this kind, and in the two I have not yet quoted there appear to be unshortened terms to express the dimensions:

[Pastura] ij quarantene lat(a) (1.8)

[Silva] dimidi- leuca lat(a) (1.9)

I have completed lata on the analogy with longa.

Consider the apparently complete leuca in the second of these examples. This form could be nominative or ablative, and in the light of my previous observation about missing marks-of-shortening, it could even be accusative (leucam), the **m** being implied by a lost superscript line: 

When we turn to the breadth of the pasture, however, "two furlongs", the ambiguity disappears. For the only plural case of the first declension whose ending contains an **e** is the nominative. So leuca could well be nominative too, and we would be acting on the principle of consistency if we then completed the other two instances of leuc- with nominative endings and harmonised the adjective dimidi- with its noun. The final solution, based on the quarantene, could therefore be as follows:

Pastura dimidi**a** leuc**a** longa et ij quarenten**e** lata.

Silva ij leuc**e** longa et dimidi**a** leuc**a** lata.

This still seems unsatisfactory; there are too many nominatives, and it is dangerous simply to assume that the scribe knew no better. At this point we wonder if a book of reference will help. Perhaps we have misremembered our grammar. But the golden rule was to regard the text in front of us as our book of reference. Is there any help to be had from the rest of the text on the folio from which this little piece was taken?

Opposite our little piece is another Domesday entry copied by the scribe, with a most helpful parallel:

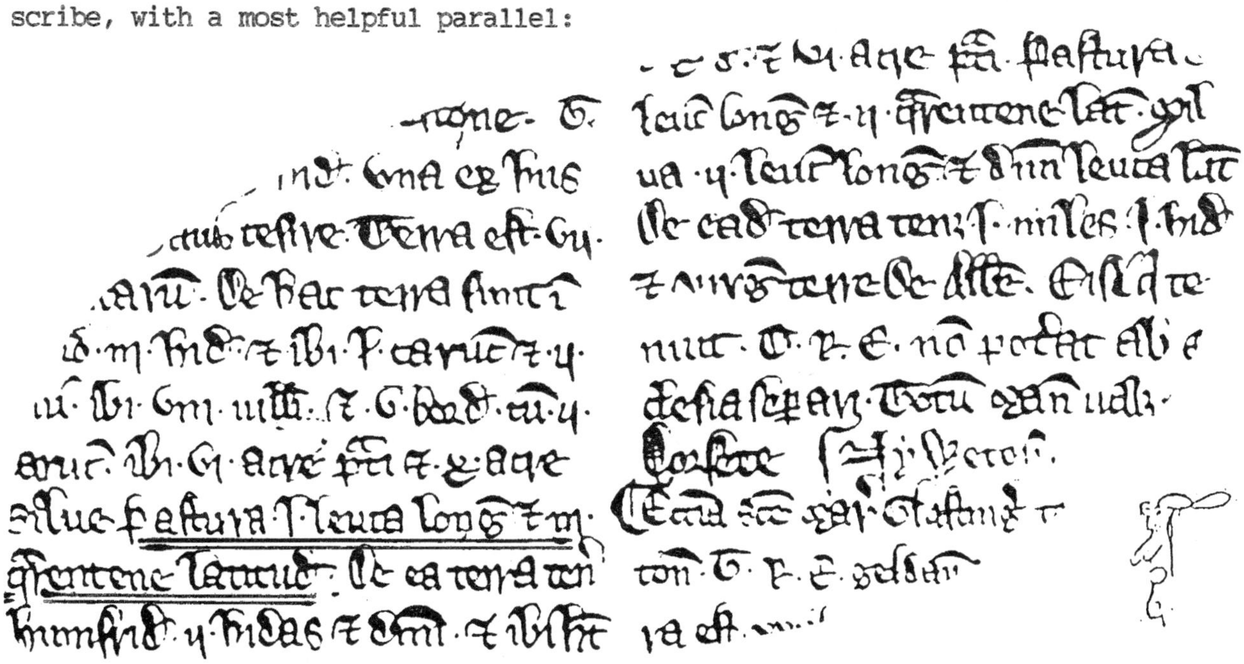

I will let you transcribe the vital section (underlined), but draw your attention to one phrase, iij quarentene latitud'. The last word puts a new complexion on the whole thing. Our original assumption about *lat-* and *long-* was reasonable, on the face of it, but possibly wrong. We do not forget that scribes were perfectly capable of elegant variation, i.e. changing the formula for variety's sake. Nevertheless, if the new text includes the noun *latitudo* (in some form) rather than the adjective *lata*, our first text may have been similarly constructed.

This new phrase means "3 furlongs **in width**". It seems best, then, to apply this unexpected clue to our original puzzle, and our final version runs thus:

Pastura [est][1] *dimidia leuca longitudine et ij quarentene latitudine*.
Silva [est] *ij leuce longitudine et dimidia leuca latitudine*

Once again, the written explanation of a piece of detective work makes it seem more complicated and long-winded than the head-work would have been.

I now offer you further practice from this particular manuscript. It comes from another section of the same folio. You will notice that this is the passage in which we found our clue.

A transcript of both texts appears in the Key.

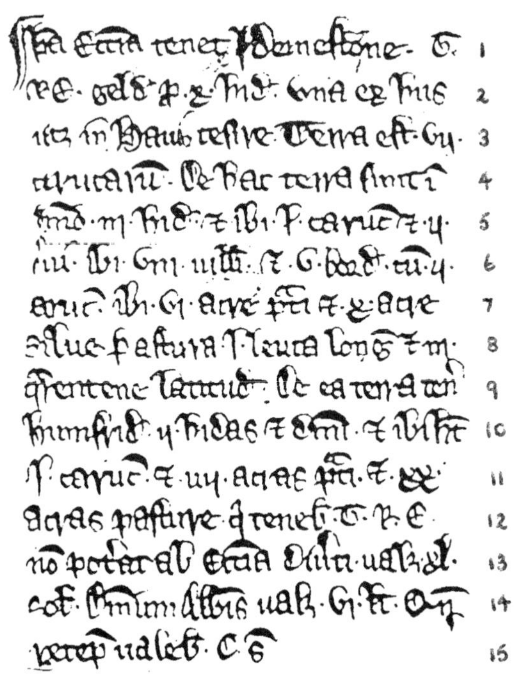

Text XXI

1. To make better grammar of the nominatives, we assume that the the verb "to be" has been omitted.

On Your Own

So far in following this beginner's book, you have tackled two distinct hands, and caught glimpses of two or three more. Now is your opportunity to extend your range. Try a copy of a charter. In accordance with my usual policy, I provide first a similar document, transcribed (Text XXII). Then follows the new text (Text XXIII). See what you can make of it.

> Dilectissimo fratri suo Ricardo Pyk' filio et heredi Ricardi Pyk', Johannes Pyk' salutem in Domino. Quia concessi, dimisi domino Galfrido Dei gracia abbati Glaston' et eiusdem loci conventui homagium et totum servicium vestrum de omnibus terris et tenementis que de me tenuistis in villa de Murlinch' pro medietate feodi unius militis, quare vobis mando et per presentes notifico quod dictis dominis abbati et conventui et eorum successoribus de cetero sitis intendentes et respondentes in omnibus, prout decet de tota tenura predicta. In cuius rei testimonium has litteras meas vobius fieri feci patentes. Dat.Glaston.die Dominica proxima ante festum Sancti Jacobi anno regni regis Edwardi xij. (23 July 1318)

TEXT XXII[1]

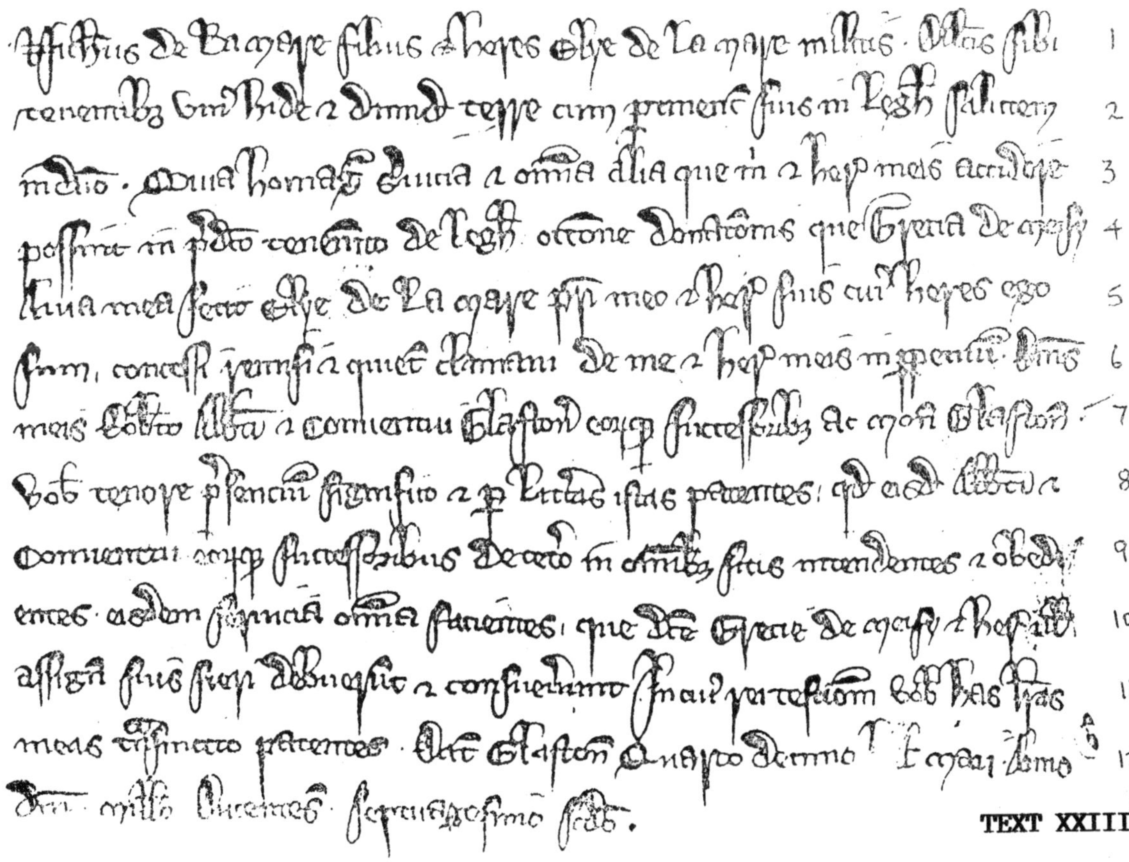

TEXT XXIII[2]

---

1. No.675 of <u>Somerset Record Society</u>, Vol.63 (1948), ed. Dom Aelred Watkin.
2. From B.L.Add.MS 17450 fol.101

Have you approached this text correctly? Did you stop to consider what was distinctive about the hand? Did you build up your own alphabet, making use of whole words? Here I offer a collection of specimens from the text against which to check your own. You will see I have included a few alternative forms. You should find that other letters are also capable of considerable variation.

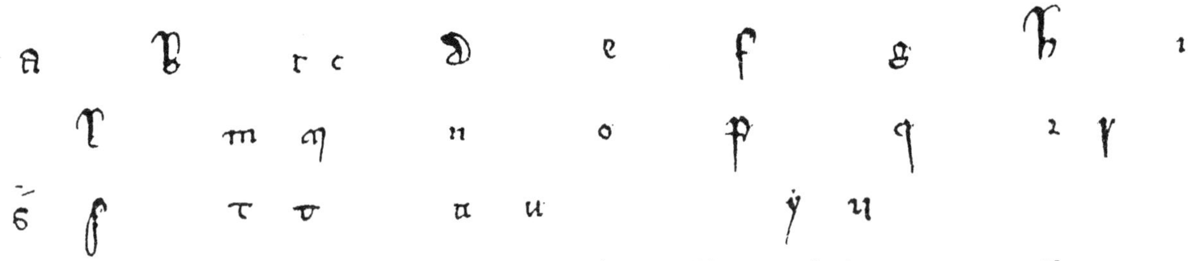

What else did you notice about this hand? Doubtless you saw the flourishes, and the spread-twig tops to **h**, **l** etc. The letters are more linked than in hands we have previously seen, and there are fewer marks of abbreviation. Indeed, the more you study this text, the more numerous you will find the whole words to be. It is not just a matter of marks being omitted from shortened words. Next, have you made use of whole words or of thoroughly familiar contractions (like pdc̄o) to attack their neighbours? Finally, have you noticed the parallels? Three times the shortened her' occurs, followed by meis(line 3), suis(line 5), meis(line 6).... Again the superscript 9 comes twice, and the meaning -us fits each time: unius hide (line 2) and cuius rei (line 11).

As a bonus I offer here a selection of instances of the main marks of abbreviation used in this text. The superscript line has not only a curve but a swelling middle, but its uses are familiar: suspension, contraction and omission. I have isolated ʒ from its context, unkindly. Which of its normal uses do you find here (-et, [-b]-us, [-q]ue) ? How is -er- shown? In the Key I offer you a transcription, printed between the lines of the text for your convenience. ON NO ACCOUNT turn to this until you have exhausted all possibilities of solving unaided any problems in the text.

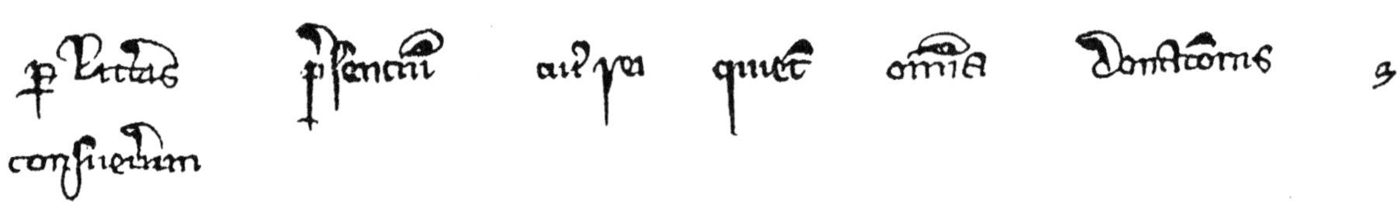

You Too Are Human

You found that charter a struggle? You made a few mistakes? Don't worry. Scribes can err, too, as we have seen. It is easy to forget that in important respects your task in deciphering and writing down the text of a medieval Latin document is parallel to that of a scribe. Like you, he was generally reading from some other text. Like him, you make a transcript of what you have read. In fact, one can gain some insight into scribal errors by reviewing errors one has made oneself. I propose to console you for the mistakes you have just made, and, more seriously, to show you some of the perils that lurk in your path, by examining actual mistakes I have made. You have already met one or two such incidents. Now I shall work more or less systematically through the chapters of this book and illustrate the particular dangers relevant to each.

When I urged you to make things easy for yourself, I especially mentioned the value of reading the (published) transcription of a similar text before tackling an unfamiliar hand. The danger here, of course, is that your mind will then be set to expect certain things, and so be liable to mis-read accordingly. The extreme form of this is when you have seen a variant version of the same text. Struggling once with a little *Inquisicio de Iuribus Ecclesie* (i.e.a dispute about a parson's rights), I remembered that the same text might be found in a published cartulary[1] of that estate. It was so, for better or worse. I found myself hesitating over this item:

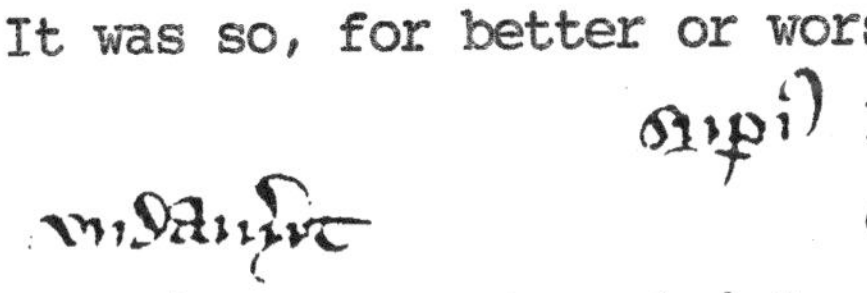

I copied from the cartulary version, and wrote down *superin-undaverint*, despite the obvious *superius*. Almost certainly *superinundaverint* gives the intended meaning, and my scribe may have made a mistake. Nevertheless, a faithful transcriber does not merely emend what seem to be incorrect items. The right course (certainly in your early days) is to record what the scribe has actually written. You can protect yourself from the suspicion of error by a parenthesised [*sic*], and offer your surmise in a footnote.

The original text of this set of charters is notoriously difficult, and it may be that my scribe, seeing a barely-legible *super-* at the end of the line, followed by some minims, supposed that he was dealing with a whole word and supplied *-ius* to make *superius*. There is a verb *undo*, *undare*, from which *undaverint* could come. However, his text, meaning "waters rise

1. Cartulary - collection or register of an estate's documents.

higher" is less apposite than the cartulary's "waters overflow" for the floods so often occurring in the region and providing the driftwood that is to be gathered.

The confusible letters are a source of some doubtful interpretations, but it might be harsh to call such events errors on the part of the transcriber. My next example is of that kind. In a published manorial survey I came across reference to a tenant, *Cristina, que fuit amica sacerdotis*. Recent reading about the celibacy of the clergy made my eyebrows rise at this "priest's female friend", especially as my classical dictionary declared that *amica* is a euphemism for *meretrix* (courtesan). My interest in this rather gratuitous bit of scandal-mongering on the part of the compiler of the survey was suitably damped when an experienced palaeographer assured me that such a usage was not known in medieval Latin. I was reminded that **c** might be **t**, the lady then being the priest's **aunt** (*amita*).

My discussion of the simpler ways of shortening words was couched in cautious terms. Nevertheless, as I have already shown, it is easy to forget the force of formulae designed to allow for exceptions to general rules. The example I have given you concerned  (*per*). On two other occasions this has been a stumbling-block. In one text I was caught out by  . All I could suppose was that it represented some part of *operio*, to cover; more precisely, part of the perfect participle passive of that verb (*opertus*, *-a*, *-um*). The difficulty was to construe it in its context. I needed a finite verb. Then the light dawned:  could mean *por-*, and the final 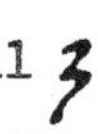 was not being used freakishly but in its common use as *-et*. ***Oportet*** was the correct reading. I will spare you the finer details of the occasion when, mindful for once of the versatility of , I read *porcum suum* where *parcum suum* (his **pound**) was clearly meant.[1]

The use of parallel texts is something I was slow to learn. That may explain the stress I have put on it. The instance of failure I recall was

---

1. Similarly, 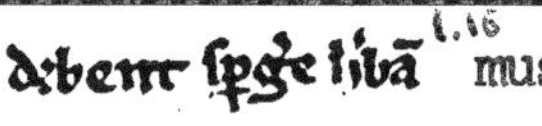 must be *debent spargere herbam* (to scatter).

the more regrettable since the word in question was clearly unfamiliar to me, whatever its precise spelling. So I should have taken more care. The text spoke of a requirement for the tenant to bring

With splendid confidence I transcribed this as virgas ad wanduram. But I could not find in the pages of Latham what wandura was, and it was the editor himself who reminded me that the two minims could represent **u**, and that wauduram would sound more or less the same as walduram. The sticks were to be brought to help in the construction of an **embankment**. You might think this example more relevant to the chapter on minims. The sting is in the tail. I had forgotten that only a folio or so previously I had successfully transcribed

as virgas ad walduram.

It is easy to neglect grammatical considerations, especially if one is unsure of the finer points. In my own case I should have remembered what I knew perfectly well when I expanded the suspended inquisicion' in this text:

My transcript read ut interessent inquisicionem iurium ecclesie. Unfortunately, I remembered too late that compounds of sum are generally followed by the dative case. It was a technical error, but an error all the same. inquisicioni was needed.

My chapter on the difficulties to do with pen-strokes touching, or not touching, i.e. with minims and with gaps generally, could be generously illustrated. For a change, I present you with a published howler. A certain headland quondam fuit drana domini. The lord's **drain**? No, but the lord's **drove**, drava. A matter of two minims.

I have to confess that, ignorant of the way meadows were organised and imagining that I had come across some technicality, I once mis-read these words at the start of a sentence:

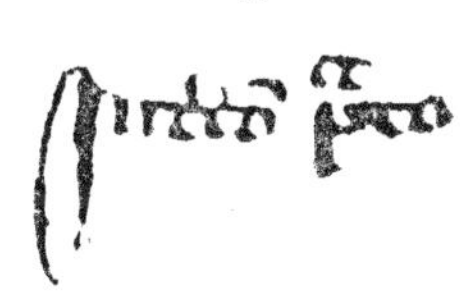

I fancied some special kind of meadow, pratum **intratum**. Perhaps it referred to the time when the livestock were allowed to **enter** the meadow after the hay is carted. My defence is that no gap is discernible before the first letter **t**. In fact, the sign of shortening above the **t** is not the -ra- sign  - that is to be seen above the **p** of prato. It is one of the marks used for -er-, and the correct reading is in tertio. The meadow under discussion had three parts: superius, inferius, and, naturally, "the third" (tertium).

It is only a kind of justice that the scribe should have committed the opposite offence a few lines later, where we find these words (how many?):

The double-**f** is really very unkind. It is the regular way of writing capital **F** and reinforces the sense of a new word imparted by the gap after in. Surely in Ferius? In this case the correct solution is obvious; this is the pratum inferius. One can only wonder what state of mind caused the scribe to write it so.

I make less apology for having in my store of errors an example of capital letter trouble. Study this longer extract:

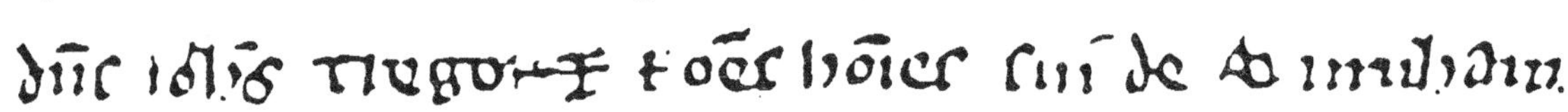

No great problem in deciphering here; even the personal names seem straightforward:

dominus Johannes Trego et omnes homines sui de ....

"Lord John Trego and all his men of/from ....." - where? Once again a little knowledge was dangerous. I knew that one of the place-names associated with this estate was Damerham or Domerham, and I convinced myself (rightly or wrongly) that I had seen it spelt Domruham. By the very common practice of careless counting of minims I saw this as the correct reading of the place-name in this text. In fact it would have to be Donruham, if the rest were correct. Alas, the capital **D** used by this scribe is the one we met in Text XX (p.101). This is not two letters (Do-) but a single capital, looking to the novice as if it is lying on its back. It is a slightly unusual **B**.[1] The pair of minims after the **r** is in fact **n**; the two minims before it are not **m** but **u**; so we have Burnham.

You will agree that I have had plentiful experience of "obstinate bits". For examples of how to tackle them rather than how NOT to tackle them, I offer one or two curiosities culled from a text already quoted (see page 82).

---

1. Here are the two capitals in proximity: 

Twice we find the otherwise unknown word *pule*:

> *si scindit lignum ad opus domini scindet j caretatam et cariabit ad curiam et habebit suum* ***pule***.

and

> *debet cariare husbote et heibote ad domos domini reparandas cum opus fuerit et habebit suum* ***pule***.

No dictionary or word-list contained anything resembling *pule*. Puzzled by this printed curiosity, I went to the British Library to inspect the manuscript. There could be no doubt. *pule* was what the manuscript said. In the second instance the word was split in half by a line-ending, but that seems irrelevant.

Now it is possible in such cases to make an informed guess. It is obvious that both passages describe duties to do with carrying wood for the lord of the manor, and they end with the clause, "and he (the tenant) shall have his.....". This must be a perquisite associated with the particular service. There are two kinds of term possible here, a general word meaning something equivalent to "perquisite", and, more probable, the specific perquisite referred to. As the service involves wood, the perquisite might well be wood, - fuel, for instance. In Latin, *fuale*. Quite how the corruption to *pule* took place is not clear, but it is a plausible enough interpretation of *pule*.

However, the editor of this text was entirely correct to transcribe what he found in the manuscript. It is for others to make what they can of his faithful rendering.

Coincidentally, the same combination of duties and rewards is the subject of another piece of faithful recording of the improbable by the editor of this text.

> *si fuerit custos boum in estate, habebit per duos dies Sabbati unam carucam de carucis domini..., et si fuerit custos boum per annum habebit j acram de blado domini, et si fuerit custos boum in hyeme in boveria domini habebit dimidium quarterium bladi pro* ***sesis*** *suis*. - 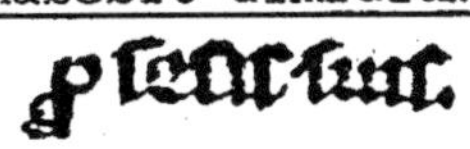

Here are spelt out the rewards for being cow-herd at various seasons: the use of the lord's plough, or some corn, "for his (the tenant's) ...." i.e. in return for his .... Here it is difficult to resist the general term "services", **serviciis,** as the intended expansion of sesis. But if so, the abbreviation is most unusual, and entirely unsupported by marks of shortening.

The medieval departures from strict classical Latin can prove a snare. Sometimes the scribe obligingly writes in full:

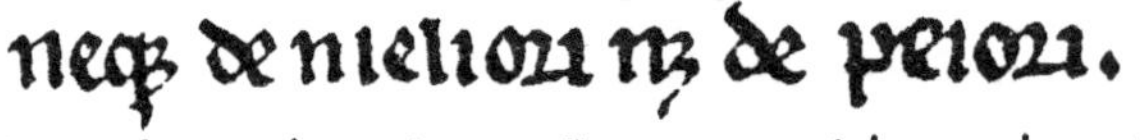

The regular ablative singular of comparatives in classical Latin ends in -e, yet here we have unmistakably -i.

Despite knowing that various such minor differences were to be found, I slipped up on this date: 

Evidently Kaln' is Kalendis, "on the first of the month". Equally evident is the month, March. My mistake was to transcribe the phrase as Kalendis Martiis, according to classical usage. Yet the manuscript **contains no** final **s.** Why not stick to the text, Martii? "On the Kalends **of** March" is congruent with modern idiom, and we have already drawn attention (page 94) to a feature of medieval Latin closely resembling the practice of modern European languages.

The mistakes and confusions I have described are, of course, chiefly those likely to be made by one who is not a fluent reader of a particular form of writing (or print) and also one who is not fluent orally in the language concerned. Such mistakes do appear from time to time in a medieval text, but more common are the mistakes due to the scribe's eye not returning to the right place in the source-text. This results in repetitions and omissions of various kinds. Awareness of this possibility may save you from the same error, and assist you in making sense of what your text offers. But at the stage that concerns us in this book, a scrupulous attention to what actually appears on the manuscript is the principal virtue.

You will doubtless have noticed that I have been lucky enough to be able to call on the help of experienced readers of medieval Latin texts from time to time. I strongly urge on you the desirability of getting to know such persons! I have never encountered anything but courtesy and helpfulness from scholars. Try the nearest Record Office, perhaps.

In the Bibliography you will find the names of those who can be consulted in the pages of their books, a small but important list.

You should by now combine a degree of confidence (based on the work you have done) with a realistic awareness that difficulties may take time to overcome. To increase your confidence I now present you with one very clear text, and to prepare you for the difficulties I add two that are a little troublesome.

The first is very repetitive, so it provides its own, massive scope for parallels and does not need a "similar" text for background. Your principal task is to transcribe field names. This means there is almost no help to be obtained from the context. It also means you have plenty of capital letters to get your teeth into. It is only fair to tell you that this scribe makes use of the Saxon 'rune' þ (the 'thorn') to represent **th**. Since field-names are mostly English, this is understandable.

The second text is also something of a list, lacking verbs. It is,in fact, part of a thirteenth century library catalogue, and it includes one or two librarian comments on the condition of the books. When you have wrestled with it as far as you are able, the Key will put you out of your misery (and also with the other texts). The important new contraction is on line 16, where āīābʒ stands for **animabus**. Notice also episcopi and patrum when you meet them.

The third text is readily recognisable as a royal writ (.....rex....). From the fact that he is a Henry and could date it by his anno xlvj^{to}, we may deduce his identity, Henry III. The hand is more like some that we have tackled, but the parchment is rough and the writing hasty. Our copy is derived from microfilm, and it demonstrates the disadvantage of reproduced text. The original MS (in the British Library) would be easier to read. Good luck!

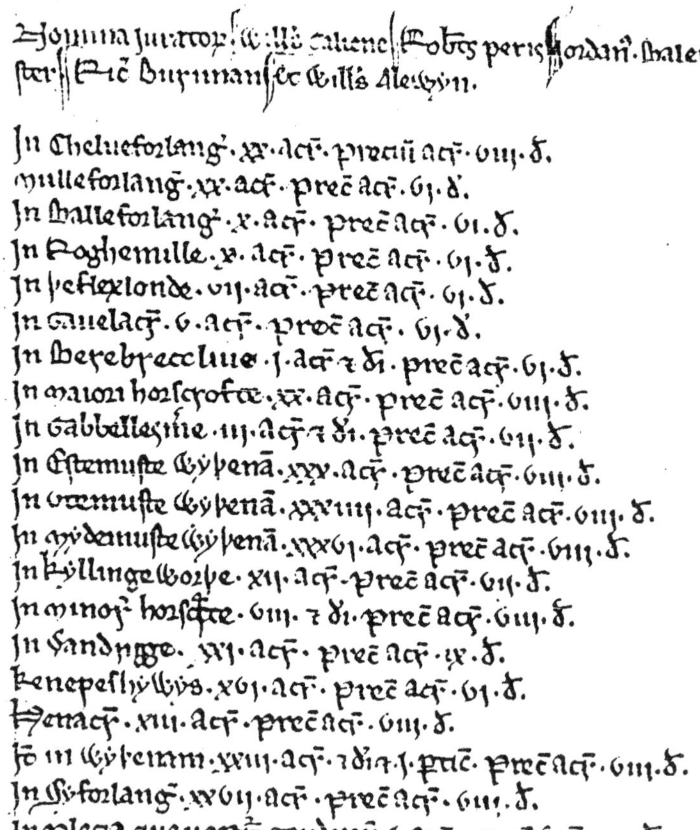

a

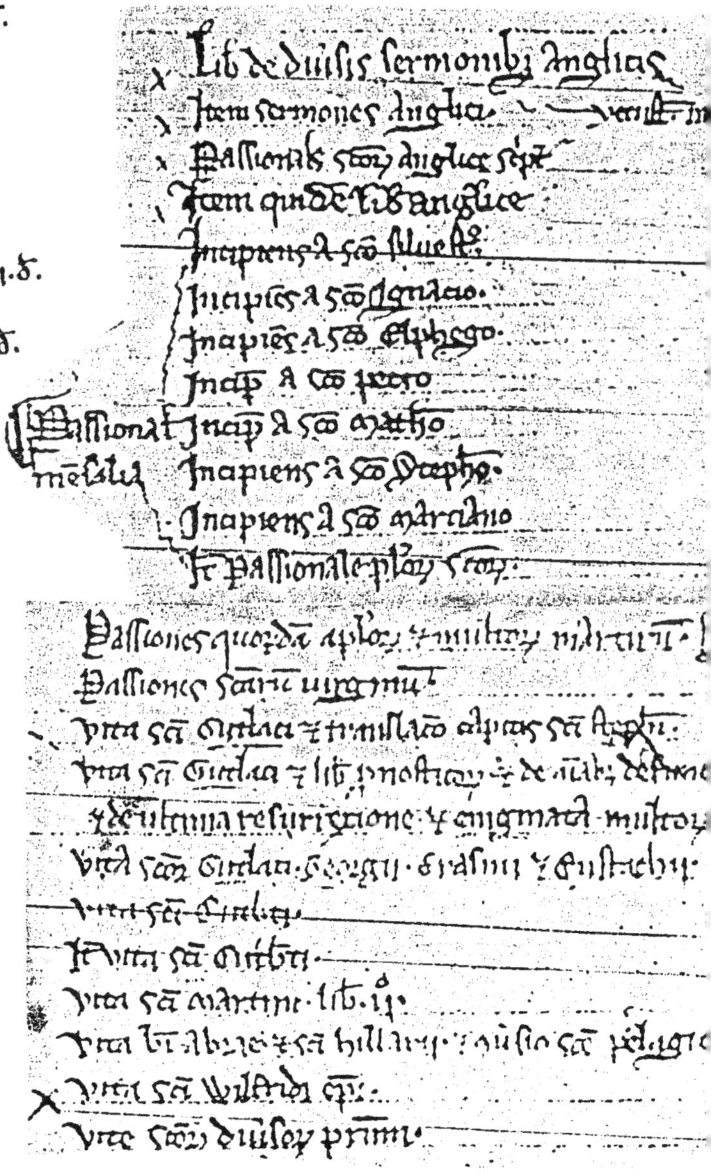

b

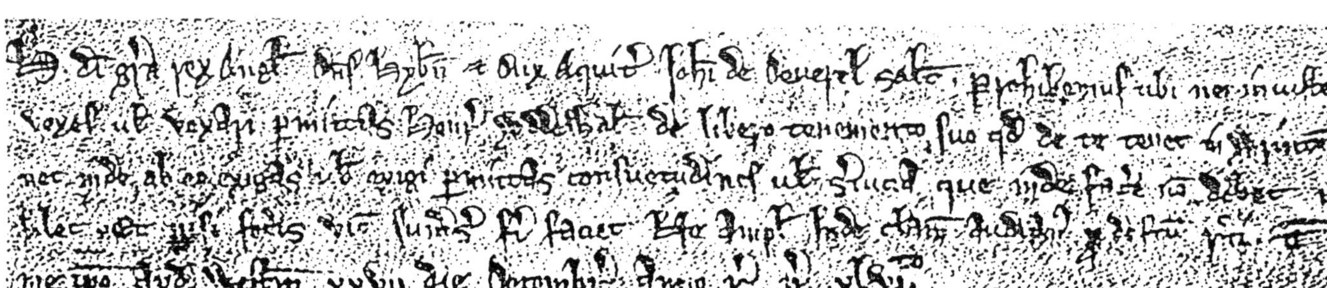

c.

TEXT XXIV

FURTHER READING

See also books recommended in the Introduction (page i)

L.C.HECTOR, The Handwriting Of English Documents (Edward Arnold 1966). Not the least of its virtues is providing sample passages with transcriptions.

CAPPELLI, Adriano, Lexicon Abbreviaturarum. Dizionario di abbreviature latine et italiane (Hoepli, Milan, 1979) Encyclopaedic, but in Italian.

DAVID IREDALE, Enjoying Archives (Phillimore 1985). A sound section on palaeography includes a chronological account of individual letters.

CHARLES JOHNSON and HILARY JENKINSON, English Court Hand A.D.1066 to 1500 (Clarendon Press 1915). A vast volume of plates combined with a scholarly volume of analysis and commentary. This also contains a thorough historical account of the letters, by no means identical with Iredale's.

M.T.CLANCHY, From Memory To Written Record (Edward Arnold 1979). The best introduction to the relation between speech and writing from 1066 to 1307.

S. HARRISON THOMPSON, Latin Bookhands Of The Later Middle Ages 1100-1500 (Cambridge University Press 1969). Superb collection of texts from Europe generally, with transcriptions of parts of each text.

JOYCE IRENE WHALLEY, The Art Of Calligraphy (Bloomsbury Books 1980). Fine black-and-white reproductions of book hands over a long period.

JOHN LANCASTER, Writing Medieval Scripts (Dryad 1988) For those who become interested in calligraphy, but containing useful information for others.

CHRISTOPHER DE HAMEL, Scribes and Illuminators (British Museum Press 1992) From their 'Medieval Craftsmen' series, it satisfies curiosity about all aspects of medieval book production. Beautifully illustrated.

ANN RYCRAFT, English Medieval Handwriting (University of York 1973) English texts reproduced and transcribed. Contains a useful, but tightly-packed, presentation of letter-forms and abbreviations found in both languages.

KEY TO EXERCISES AND EXAMPLES

page 27 lavare, arare, ire, falcare;
levare, serclare, cariare, invenire, venire.

page 30

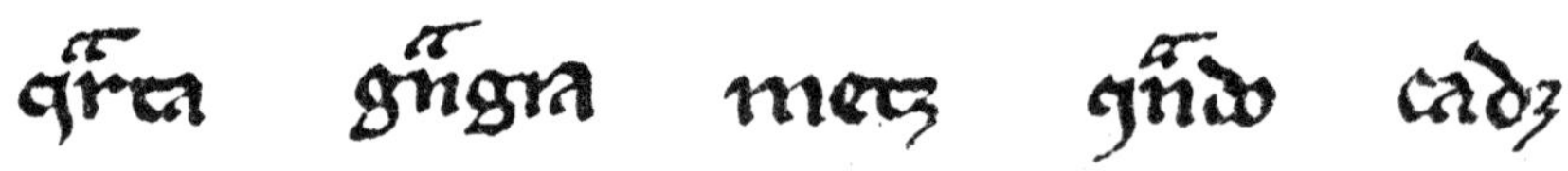

page 32 levare cu manco falcis sue
manc^9 no tangz tram
si manc^{9}frangatur

page 33

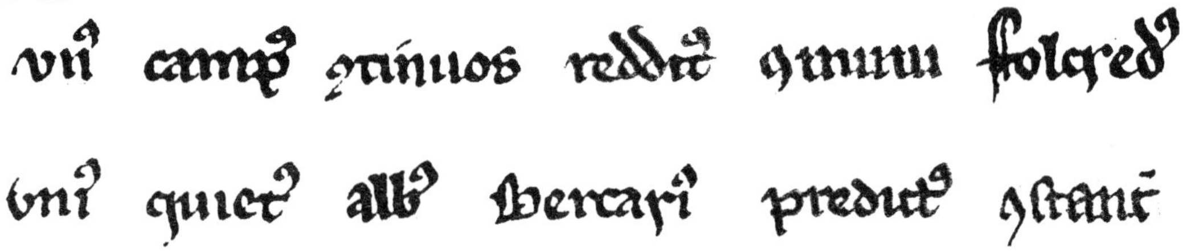

page 43

1. The 8 sounds can be heard in these words:
   banana bather man many fall what daring

2. Doubtless conventional accounts of Latin simplify the issue. Beyond question we hear that vowels can be 'short' or 'long'. Also it is to be presumed that to all intents and purposes we hear the same sound in these:
   Kalendae cecenisse quisque (the -u- = /w/)

3. I think at least four categories of **/** can be identified:
   (a) to indicate a part of a word interrupted by the ending of a line (see pages 29 and 53).
   (b) accompanying certain instances of the letter **i**, as in invenire (line 29 of the text).
   (c) in association with what looks like a rather subdued full-stop, as after tassus in line 38.
   (d) less easy to categorise, as it is a one-off, is the **/** on line 16 before debent. A second look at your examples of type (c) might enable you to embrace this odd instance.

4. Three of these words carry clear images in their etymology, - scraping, pricking dots, drawing a criss-cross. 'Obliterate' seems more abstract, but Chambers Twentieth Century Dictionary gives the clue. The prefix ob- implies covering **over** letters in the way that only a blot can do. These terms all reflect medieval methods of what may be simply termed 'deletion'. i.e. The scribes had several means of achieving a single aim.

page 46 festum, denarios, quieta. cervisia, boum, semen, acuendas, cullardum

page 48 The scribe's version of the suspended words..

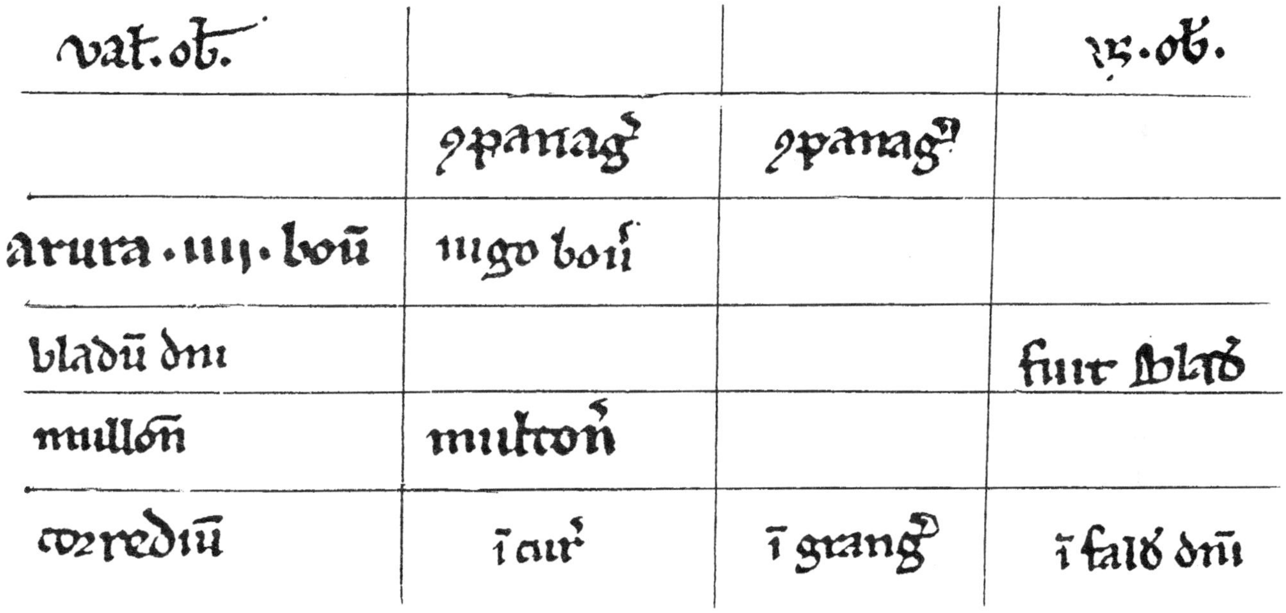

page 48 Completion of the suspended words.

obolus			obolus
	companagio*	companagio*	
boum	boum		
bladum			bladum
mullonem	multonem		
corredium	curia*	grangia*	falda

* In the MS the final -**i** of the stem was dropped as well as the grammatical suffix. The mark of abbreviation embraces both omissions.

page 55 According to 'rule': superscript ᵃ = -ra-. acm̄ = acram
superscript ¯ = -m/n-. acr̄ = acram

Unusual : You would expect acr̄m to mean acrram (a surplus r).
Superscript line over a consonant means, Guess. acr̄ = acr ??.

page 57 nil habere, quolibet anno, omnes qui, et hac arura.

page 59 boveria, ter in anno, non tanget terram, fuerit,
poterit levare, plura averia,
ad yvernagium, ad acram domini quam araverit.

page 60 suum averoc scilicet t'm herbe quantum....
in illa herba
si mancus frangatur, perdet herbam

page 62 autumpno, seminatore, inveniet, ultima.

page 63

ad custum, per corigiam, post nonam;
unam garbam, herciatorem suum;
habebit illum caseum, inveniet seminatorem, dominus pascet illum,
facere mullonem.

page 66 dominus pascet illum et herciatorem suum semel
habere de dono domini cum vicinis suis ij d.
si dominus nullum cullardum vel multonem in falda sua haberet
debet metere quolibet die in autumpno dimidiam acram

page 68 Isabella, Sarra, Weman, Medgavel, Lovebonde, Frymora
Folcredus, Johannis, Sancte, Lardarium, Magister, Willelmus

page 71 ....j acram scilicet viij perticas
.... versus meridiem..........habet unum angulum

page 72 This cursive R has a flourish back from the vertical stroke, - cf.:

page 73 Alicia, Alditha, Adam, Adam
Domini, Drofacr.., David, Digun
Cristina, Cullardo, Cetera, Cherm
Gulam, Galfridus, Glaston', Galfridus
Hurn', Henricus, herding(in fact a lower case **h**)
Nicholaus, Notandum, Nigelli
Quod, Quicunque, Quilibet, Quatuor
Omnes(or Omnis), Emma, Eodem, Osmundus
Predictus, Pannagium, Pere, Paulus
Turkel, Toky, Tenentes, Tutteyete
Ysabella

page 74 Bladum, Broc, Johannes Bul, Brodforlang'
Bichelak, Bernard', Bere, Bere, Blundus, Baldewinus

page 76 venire, tantumd[em], stramine, pertinet
Et habebit illum caseum qui factus fuerit in curia domini ultimo die
sex predictorum dierum quibus debet falcare et secundum meliorem
cullardum in.......... cum vicinis suis
Et debet cariare bladum .... fuerit cariandum

page 79 araverit , cervisio, dimidiam acram (See pages 52 and 71 for help.)

page 91 xlviij handenas per annum que valent ij s. Item arat et herciat ad yvernagium iiij acras et duas partes dimidie acre. Et arat et herciat in ybernagium duas acres et dimidiam et ducet semen quod valet ij s. ij d. ob. Et metet ij acras et habebit iiij garbas et valet iiij d. ob. Item cariabit fenum et bladum domini per iiij dies quod valet xvi d. Summagiabit quod valet per annum xvi. Item falcat et levat quod valet per annum ob. et habebit medmete quod valet ob. Item metet arundinem quolibet anno si necesse fuerit quod valet per annum ob. Et si Dominus habeat novam domum faciendam erit ad muros faciendos quod valet ob. Item fossabit apud Mordich' semper secundo anno quod valet ob. Et trahet vina domini quod valet per annum ob. Item fossabit apud Thurlmere per dimidiam diem semper secundo anno quod valet per anum ob. Item claudet in parco de Pulton' semper quarto anno j perticam et valet per annum iiij d.

page 98

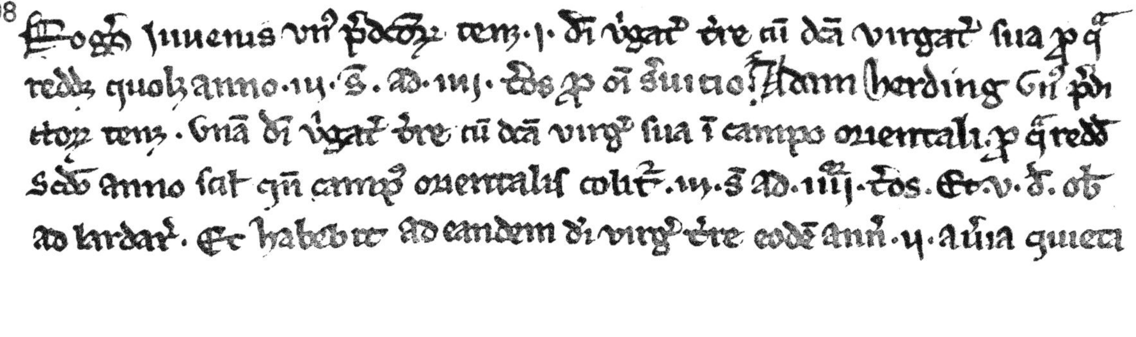

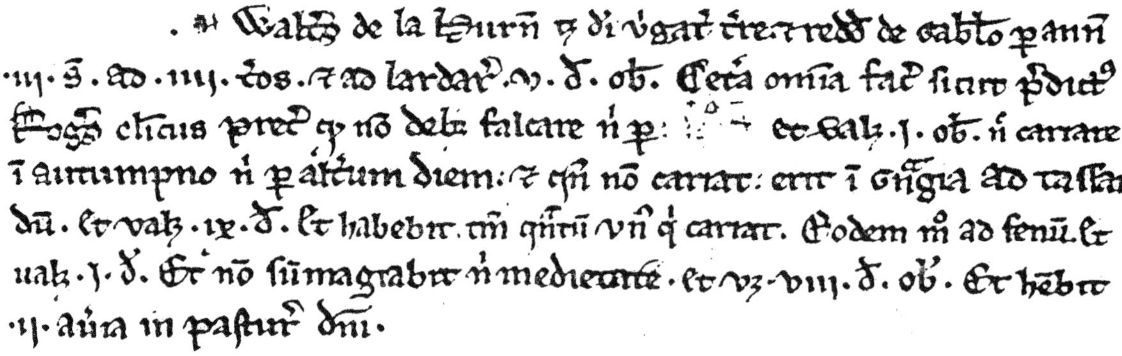

page 101 (Text XX)

1. Ipsa ecclesia tenet Deverel. Tempore Regis Edwardi gelda-
2. vit pro x hidis. Terra est ix carucarum
3. De hac terra sunt in dominio v hide et
4. ibi iij caruce et ij servi. Ibi xiiij villani
5. xxiiij bordarii et xij cotarii cum vj carucis.
6. Ibi iij molendini reddunt xiiij solidos
7. et x den. et vj acre prati Pastura dimidia
8. leuca longitudine et ij quarentene latitudine. Sil-
9. va ij leuce longitudine et dimidia leuca latitudine.
10. De eadem terra tenet j miles j hidam
11. et virgatam terre de Abbate. Eisi qui te-
12. nuit tempore Regis Edwardi non poterat ab ec-
13. clesia separari. Totum manerium valet xij libri.

page 106 (Text XXI)

1. Ipsa Ecclesia tenet Idemestone. T.
2. R.E. geldavit pro x hidis. Una ex hiis
3. jacet in Hans tesire [Hantescire?]. Terra est vij
4. carucarum. De hac terra fuerunt in
5. dominio iij hide. Et ibi j caruca et ij
6. servi. Ibi viij villani et v bordarii cum ij
7. carucis. Ibi vj acre prati et x acre
8. silve. Pastura j leuca longitudine et iij
9. quarentene latitudine. De ea terra tenet
10. Humfridus ij hidas et dimidiam et ibi habet
11. j carucam et iiij acras prati et xx
12. acras pasture. Qui tenebat T.R.E.
13. non poterat ab ecclesia diverti. Valet xl
14. sol. Dominium Abbatis valet vj li. Quando
15. recepit valebat C s.

p.107

Nicholaus de la Mare, filius et heres Elye de la Mare militis, dilectis sibi
tenentibus unius hide et dimidie terre cum pertinenciis suis in Legh salutem
in Domino.Quia homagia servicia et omnia alia que michi et heredibus meis accidere
possint in predicto tenemento de Legh occasione donacionis que Grecia de Meisy
avia mea fecit Elye de la Mare patri meo et heredibus suis cuius heres ego
sum concessi remisi et quietum clamavi de me et heredibus meis in perpetuum dominis
meis Roberto Abbati et conventui Glaston eorunque successoribus ac monasterio Glaston
vobis tenore presencium significo et per litteras istas patentes quod eisdem abbati et
conventui eorunque successoribus de cetero in omnibus sitis intendentes et obedi-
entes eisdem servicia omnia facientes que dicte Grecie de Meisy et heredibus vel
assignatis suis fieri debuerunt et consueverunt.In cuius rei testimonium vobis has litteras
meas transmitto patentes. Dat. Glaston Quarto decimo Kal. Maij anno
domini millesimo ducentesimo septuagentesimo secundo.

TEXT XXIII - Transcribed

page 114 <u>neque de meliori neque de peiori</u>
<u>Kalendis .... Anno domini m^{o} CC lxj^{o}</u>

page 116 TEXT XXIV

(a) Nomina juratorum: Willelmus Galiene, Robertus Peris, Jordanus Balet, Walterus
Ster, Ricardus Buriman et Willelmus Alewyn.

In Chelveforlang' xx acre, precium acre viij den.
Mulleforlang' xx acre, precium acre vj den.
In Balleforlang' x acre, precium acre vj den.
In Roghemille x acre, precium acre vj den. [or Roghenulle]
In *Theflexlonde vij acre, precium acre vj den.
In Gavelacra v acre, precium acre vj den.
In Berebrecclive j acra et dimidia, precium acre vj den.
In maiori horsecrofte xx acre, precium acre viij den.
In Gabellesmere iij acre et dimidia, precium acre vij den.
In Estemuste Wyth*enam xxx acre, precium acre viij den.
In utemuste Wythenam* xxxiiij acre, precium acre viij. [den.]
In mydemuste Wythenam* xxxvj acre, precium acre viij den.
In Kyllingeworthe xij acre, precium acre vij den.
In minori horsecrofte viij et dimidia, precium acre viij den.
In Sandrugge xxj acre, precium acre ix den.
Kenepeshywys xvj acre, precium acre vj den.
Henacra xiij acre, precium acre viij den.
Item, in Wythenam* xxiij acre et dimidia
et j perticam, precium acre viij [den.]
In Syforlang' xxvij acre, precium acre viij den.
In plecia que vocatur gardinum j acra, precium acre xij [den.]

*Some authorities find it helpful to <u>print</u> a 'thorn' to represent the Saxon rune found in manuscript, rather than indicate its significance by the conventional **th**. I would recommend simple transciption into **th** with some footnote of explanation. This enables the text to be read straightforwardly and yet the distinctive letter-form to be recorded.

(See page 115 para 4)

(p.116)

(b) Liber de diversis sermonibus anglicis.
Item sermones anglici.)vetusti, inutiles.
Passionalis sanctorum anglice scriptus)
Item quidem[1] liber anglice
Incipiens a sancto Silvestro.
Incipiens a sancto Ignacio.
Incipiens a sancto Elphego.
Incipiens a sancto Petro
[2]Incipiens a sancto Mathaeo
Incipiens a sancto Stephano.
Incipiens a sancto Marciano
Item Passionale plurimorum sanctorum.

Passiones quorundam apostolorum et multorum martirum. Legibile.
Passiones sanctarum virginum.
Vita sancti Gutlaci et translacio capitis sancti Stephani.
Vita sancti Gutlaci et liber pronosticorum et de animabus defunctorum.
et de ultima resurrexione et enigmata multorum.
Vita sanctorum Gutlaci, Georgii, Erasmi et Eustachii.
Vita sancti Cutberti.
Item, vita sancti Cutberti.
Vita sancti Martini, libri ij^{o}.
Vita beati Abrae et sancti Hillarii et conversio sancte Pelagie.
Vita sancti Wilfridi episcopi.
Vite sanctorum diversorum patrum.

---

1. Should be quidam.
2. Passionalia mensalia on left-hand side of this column.

(p.116)

(c) Henricus dei gracia rex Anglie dominus Hybernie et dux Aquitanie
Johanni de Deverel salutem. Prohibemus tibi ne iniuste
vexes vel vexari permittas Henricum Wddewale de libero tenemento
suo quod de te tenet in Wrinton
nec inde ab eo exigas vel exigi permittas consuetudines vel
servicia que inde facere non debet nec
solet. Et nisi feceris, vicecomes Sumerset fieri faciet Ne
amplius inde clamium audiamus pro defectu recti. Teste
me ipso apud Westm. xxvij die Decembr' anno regni nostri xlvj^{to}

SUMMARY OF SIGNS OF ABBREVIATION

(The page references are to the discussions in the main text.)
(Most of the items are also mentioned on pages 102-108.)
(I use the EQUALS sign to mean "is usually read as".)

Working from the most specific and the most reliable:

⁊ = et, - usually known as "Tironian et" (p.36).
 = post- (see p.63)
ꝓ = pro- (see p.31)
 = pre- (see p.60)

ꝯ = con-/com- at the beginning of words (p.33)
ꝝ a suspended **r**, commonly but not necessarily signifies -rum.(page 48)

ꝑ = per- (see page 31) and also -par- and -por- (see page 110)
ꝫ = -et most commonly, in verbs and their derivatives
like quilib**et** (pp.31,86).
bꝫ = -bus in nouns and adjectives etc. (pp.28-31).
ꝫ = -ue after **q**, and sometimes ꝫ = -que (p.86).

Superscript ꝰ means -us- (p.32).
Any superscript letter merely declares that letter to be one of those that have been omitted (p.57)
Superscript '**a**', as the sign  is called, generally indicates -ar- (rarely -ra-). With **q** it means -ua- (pp.29-31).
Superscript 'twist' commonly means -er- (p.58), but can also be a non-specific sign of omission (p.47).
Superscript line commonly indicates the omission of **m** or **n** (p.31), but is also used as a general or non-specific sign of shortening (p.47).

Non-specific signs of omission include the 'twist' and the superscript line (see above), as well as the hook and the flourish - which is probably an elaborated 'twist' (p.47).
Any word can be abbreviated in multiple ways, and a sign may indicate such overall contraction as well as some specific element.
Thus debet can contract to 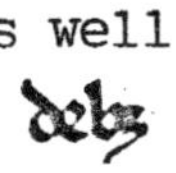 , or more thoroughly to  (page 28).

SUPPLEMENT TO SUMMARY OF SIGNS OF ABBREVIATION

It is doubtful whether any text-book contains a complete account of the various signs used over a period of about a thousand years, - at least, an account that would satisfy all critics. The list on page 125 emerged from our study of a single page of a particular text, and is necessarily far from comprehensive. Below I draw your attention to some of the ways in which its scope is limited.

⁊, the Tironian <u>et</u> (and) is also written without a bar: 7.
(The ampersand, &, is rare.)

ˀ can mean <u>-re-</u> (as well as <u>-er-</u>) in positions other than p̃ (<u>pre-</u>).

/ occurs regularly across capital **R** to mean <u>Rex</u>. It also survived, fossil-like, in medical prescriptions, ℞ for <u>Recipe</u> (Take...).

In C12th MSS ꝫ looked like a modern semi-colon with a tail: ꝫ.

Superscript '**i**' commonly means <u>-ri-</u> (rarely <u>-ir-</u>);
Superscript '**r**' commonly means <u>-ur-</u> (rarely <u>-ru-</u>);
Therefore t^{i2}rabit = <u>triturabit</u>.

÷ = <u>est</u> occurs especially in 11th-12th. ẽe means <u>esse</u>.

Generally look out for superscript signs that are formed by continuing a letter upwards uninterruptedly into the sign. They are tricky.

CHAPTER SUMMARIES

(NB 1 Summaries of Things to Remember, NOT of all the chapter contains.)

(NB 2 After one reference, repeated matters are not mentioned here again.)

Three categories of material:

Interpretation of signs and letters

PROCEDURES TO FOLLOW

Useful maxims to bear in mind

+ my headings, explanations etc

Ch.1 On Making Things Easy For Yourself

Practical Problems.....USE PHOTOCOPIED (AND ENLARGED) TEXTS.
NUMBER THE LINES OF (COPIED) TEXT.

Unfamiliar language....FIRST STUDY MATERIAL SIMILAR TO CHOSEN TEXT
- ALREADY TRANSCRIBED &/OR TRANSLATED.

The MS you are reading is your reference-book.

Ch.2 Whole Words And What To Do About Them

Because abbreviation is such a big problem, BEGIN WITH WHOLE WORDS.

Ch.3 Building Up An Alphabet

WRITE THE SCRIPT YOURSELF.

ATTEND TO DETAILS OF EACH LETTER - HEIGHT (a s v w);
- DIRECTION OF STROKE;
- ALTERNATIVE FORMS OF A LETTER, (a g m r u v).

NOTE LETTERS THAT COULD BE MISTAKEN FOR EACH OTHER (a/ꝺ c/t s/f).

CHECK YOUR ATTEMPTS AGAINST WHAT THE SCRIBE WROTE.

Ch.4 Some Rules Of Shortening

USE WHOLE WORD TO INTERPRET ADJACENT PART-WORD.

HAVE A GO AT NUMERALS (last **i** of a row is written as **j**).

ATTACK TRANSCRIBING PIECEMEAL - PREFERABLY ON "SPACED" COPY OF TEXT.

Prelim.inferences - **Grammatical knowledge yields dividends.**
- ꝺꝫ seems to be a verb followed by the infinitive.
- USE DICTIONARY TO FIND DECLENSION & GENDER.
- DEDUCE NOUN CASE-ENDING FROM PRECEDING PREPOSITION.
- **Singular/plural is not always easy to decide.**

So far,-

ʒ is not **z**.....; it occurs in **dʒ** and **vʒ** .

- occurs in noun, preposition and adjective.

ʼ occurs mostly in nouns.

Small sample demands tentative tone.

As a result of two pages of close study,-

COLLECT SIMILAR INSTANCES AND SEEK GENERAL PATTERN.

EXPLOIT ANY WHOLE WORDS.

LOOK AROUND FOR FULLER (OR COMPLETE) VERSION OF SHORTENED WORD.

FORMULATE A GENERAL RULE OR MEANING.

REFER BACK TO THE "SIMILAR TEXT" (cf.p.3) FOR GUIDANCE.

LOOK FOR INSTANCES TO CONFIRM OR CHALLENGE YOUR DEDUCTION.

ALWAYS ATTEND TO THE GRAMMAR OF THE WORDS UNDER THE LENS.

Meaning and context are crucial.

Reasonable deductions from our analyses so far: [see page 31]

Ch.5 The Use Of Parallel Expressions

LOOK OUT FOR PHRASES OR CLAUSES REPEATED IN NEAR-IDENTICAL FORM.

9 on the line means con- or com-.

superscript **9** means -us-.

Ch.6 Back To The Transcript

CONTINUE ADDING TO THE TRANSCRIPT, PIECEMEAL, -

IF POSSIBLE NOT MIXING SUCCESSIVE STAGES OF THIS INPUT.

Points to notice while transcribing;

⁊ looks as if it must mean et (and).

dns, dni, dno - parts of dominus.

ī must be in, so the rule about superscript line includes **m** AND **n**.

YOU COULD NOW BEGIN TO TRANSCRIBE PARTS OF WORDS, TENTATIVELY.

YOU COULD ALSO TRY TO DEDUCE ENDINGS, - ON GRAMMATICAL GROUNDS.

The vicious circle : the context you lean on is itself abbreviated!

Ch.7 Not One-For-One Correspondence

One sign has several meanings; several signs can mean the same.

STUDY THE CONTEXT (MEANING & GRAMMAR).

ATTEND TO THE POSITION OF THE SIGN ON THE PAGE.

Three kinds of abbreviation

Chopping off the end (= Suspension)

Omitting a letter or a row of letters from mid-word (= Omission)

Omitting more-than-one row of letters from a word (= Contraction)

The "most troublesome" fact

Some signs are specific, some are non-specific;

the same sign can be both, specific or non-specific.

Also: The light oblique stroke has several uses.

Scribes employed several methods of deleting.

ch.8 A Grammatical Chapter

Temporarily, IGNORE DIFFERENCES BETWEEN SIGNS (temporarily, I say).

Three elementary rules:

The case-ending of a noun may be fixed by the preceding preposition, or by its relation to the verb (subject - verb - object), and an adjective agrees with its noun in case, gender and number.

Sundry observations!

LOOK OUT FOR WORDS SPLIT AT THE END OF A LINE (SOME MARKED BY A /).

The principle of 'redundancy' in language provides extra clues.

BEWARE OF IMPOSSIBLE DEDUCTIONS (E.G." ıllıī = illos").

ch.9 Four Signs

Just to mean that a word is 'suspended': the hook, twist, line and flourish - and also the oblique line (with 2÷).

Common equivalents can blind us to other possibilities.

ch.10 Some Problems Of Suspension

More grammatical reasoning

USE THE USUAL GRAMMATICAL RULES (see ch.8) TO TACKLE GERUNDIVES,

- G.OF OBLIGATION OR G.ATTRACTION.

USE WIDER KNOWLEDGE AND OTHER READING TO SETTLE SINGULAR/PLURAL.

When grammar cannot help, there is some comfort:

The "Rule of Thumb"

The commonest words are the most likely to be shortened.

EXPLOIT THE WHOLE SENTENCE: CONTEXT IS NOT JUST A FEW WORDS.

LOOK OUT FOR MISLEADING HALF-WORDS AT THE BEGINNING OF A LINE.

BEWARE OF DEVELOPING BLINKERED EXPECTATIONS.

Scribes can make mistakes.

Both the twist and the line can be mere marks of suspension.

ch.11 Omission and Contraction

- **Grammar seldom helps with middles-of-words.**

The "Useful Habit" of Scribes

Scribes use alternative abbreviated-forms in proximity.

MAKE USE OF THESE ALTERNATIVES.

LOOK OUT ALSO FOR THE WORD WRITTEN IN FULL!

TRY THE CROSSWORD PUZZLERS' APPROACH.

When even the context gives inadequate help...

MAKE USE OF "SPECIFIC" SIGNS OF SHORTENING:

(i) Superscript letter implies omission of that letter + ...

ch.12 = ...(ii) The Twist frequently means -er-.

But, **the Twist does not always mean -er-.**

EXPLOIT ANY BALANCED SENTENCES OR ANTITHESES.

ch.13 = ...(iii) The Superscript Line (commonly meaning **m** or **n**).

A common occurrence is  meaning -cio-.

The line can stand above a letter or several letters

The omitted material may belong before the mark, after it, or both.

The line often cuts through a letter's 'ascender'.

Among common (i.e.much curtailed) words are sum & habere

[ is a one-off; it means post.]

ch.14 Capital Matters

LOOK OUT FOR IRREGULAR USE OF CAPITALS AND LOWER-CASE LETTERS.

Scribes were inconsistent in spelling names.

Confusibles include R/K, A/D, C/G, H/N, E/O/Q.

Some capitals come to lie on their backs, e. g. B.

ch.15 Pen Strokes

BEWARE WRONGLY JOINED/SEPARATED MINIMS.

Count the minims, BUT ALSO ATTEND TO MEANING AND GRAMMAR.

REMEMBER THE SECOND STROKE OF **h** MAY COUNT AS A 'MINIM'.

CONTEXT MUST GUIDE WHEN THE CHOICE IS cc / ct / tt / tc.

t has an 'ascender' when it follows 'tall' **s**.

BE PATIENT IN DISENTANGLING SQUASHED OR OVERLAPPING LETTERS.

Ch.16 Obstinate Bits

ALWAYS REFER BACK IF THE SCRIBE INVITES YOU TO.

BY ALL MEANS USE ANALOGY, BUT CIRCUMSPECTLY.

REMEMBER A SIGN (e.g.¯) CAN BE SPECIFIC OR NON-SPECIFIC.

ʒ can mean -et or a row ending -et; it can also mean -ue or -que

Ch.17 Punctuation

Medieval punctuation was:

- used to indicate pauses;
- used to separate numerals from surrounding text;
- used to emphasise that a word is abbreviated;
- a sign that the scribe needed to rest his hand.

Our notion of a 'sentence' is unhelpful.

Et was freely used to introduce further information (and to imply continuity) with either a capital **E** or a large **e**.

USE MODERN PUNCTUATION AND SACRIFICE 'FIDELITY'(?).

Ch.18 Not Strictly Classical (hardly capable of further summarisation)

Ch.19 Why Bother?

Signs of shortening may not be necessary, but they are useful.

Ch.20 Another Hand, Another Text

The superscript line acquires a curve.

BE PREPARED TO FIND A HOME FOR INSERTIONS, CORRECTIONS ETC.

BE PREPARED TO ABANDON YOUR FIRST HYPOTHESIS.

REMEMBER THAT 'NORMAL' EQUIVALENTS ARE SOMETIMES INAPPROPRIATE.

BE PREPARED FOR NEW FEATURES IN NEW SCRIBAL HANDS.

Double letters often overlap.

Ch.21 On Your Own (This contains no new teaching points.)

Ch.22 You Too Are Human

The mind can be too well prepared (e.g.by reading "similar text").

Phonetic spelling may sometimes provide a clue to names.

WHEN ALL SENSE FAILS, RECORD THE 'NONSENSE' IN YOUR TRANSCRIPT.

Context sometimes permits either a generic or a specific term.

EXPECT MEDIEVAL USAGE, BUT LOOK OUT FOR CLASSICAL USAGE TOO.

A new 'letter': the thorn (þ).

New common contractions to watch out for: prum, epi, aiabz.

Appendix A - The MS from which Text IV was transcribed.

Witts auenel ten. j. virgat' tre 7 reddet i sabto p ann. iiij. s. sat ad q'lz tin xij. d. Et ad lardar' ad Natale. xij. d. Et d3 adiuuare ad lauand 7 tondend oues dni. 7 v3 h. ij. d. Et d3 Warectare ad festu sci Johis bapt p. viij. bob3 vij. acr. ut si pauciores bou huit. Warectabit p uno q'q' boue octaua pte. vij. acrar. Et tantumde d3 arare dno stati p' festu bi Martini. Et v3 h aru si octo bou huit. v. s. x. d. Et p haru: d3 hre boues suos cu bob3 dni. i pastu dni. Et d3 sarclare bladu dni una die i estate cu. j. hoie us3 nonam. Et si dns illu pascet. us3 uespam. 7 v3 ij. ob. Et d3 falcare ptu dni p ij. dies. 7 dns illu pasc3 bis i die cu pane de fro 7 caseo. 7 v3 ei falcatio. vj. d. Et d3 leuare ad custu suu q'ntu falcauit. Et v3 h. viij. d. Et d3 cariare p' dem fenu i cur' dni. 7 v3 cariatio. vij. d. ob. Et d3 mete bladu dni ad pces p. iij. dies i autupno cu. ij. hoib3 7 dns illos pasc3 bis i die. s3 pmis. ij. dieb3 cu pan 7 cas. Et tcia die i pan 7 cas ad non. 7 sero: in pan. ceru. 7 carn. i cur' dni. Et q'rta die si op' fuit. d3 mete cu. j. hoie. 7 dns illu pasc3. 7 v3 messio sua. xiiij. d. Et d3 cariare bladu dni 7 n hre. 7 v3 cariatio ei. ij. s. 7 d3 sumagiare corrediu dni de burgo quociens op' fuit. 7 v3 q'lz cariatio. ij. d. 7 d3 cariare buscam ad cur' 9 aduente dni. 7 v3 q'lz cariatio. ij. d. Et d3 uenire bis i anno ad pl' dni cu bob3 suis. Et v3 ara eide. viij. d. si viij. bou hat. Et d3 cariare uictualia dni ad ponte de stan. Et v3 h. x. d. Et d3 cariare lanam 7 cas dni ubi nece fuit i eode Com. ut apd Wyntebom. ut apd Aleberg. Et valz h. j. d. ob.

Appendix B - TRANSLATION OF TEXT IV

William Avenel holds 1 virgate of land and pays in rent per year 4sh., that is, 12d at every term-day, and for larder-rent 12d at Christmas. And he has to help at washing and shearing the lord's sheep, and this is worth 2d. And he has to plough for the fallow at the feast of St John the Baptist 7 acres for the 8 oxen he has, and if he has fewer [than 8] oxen he shall plough for the fallow one eighth part of 7 acres for every ox that he has. And he has to plough the same amount for the lord immediately after the Feast of St Martin, and this ploughing, if he has 8 oxen, is worth 5sh. 10d. And in return for this ploughing he has to have his oxen in the lord's pasture with the lord's oxen. And he has to weed the lords crop for one day in summer with 1 man until noon, and until evening if the lord feeds him, and this is worth ½d. And he has to mow the lord's meadow for 2 days, and the lord shall feed him twice a day with wheat bread and cheese, and his mowing is worth 6d. And he has to make, at his own cost, as much [hay] as he has mown, and this is worth 8d. And he has to cart the said hay to the lord's courtyard, and the carrying is worth 7½d. And he has to reap the lord's corn as boon-work for 3 days in autumn with 2 men, and the lord shall feed them twice a day, that is, on the first 2 days with bread and cheese, and on the third day with bread and cheese at noon and later with bread, meat and ale in the lord's courtyard. And on the fourth day, if there is need, he shall reap with one man and the lord shall feed him, and his reaping is worth 14d. And he has to cart the lord's corn, and receive nothing, and his carting is worth 2 sh. And he has to convey by pack-animal the lord's provisions from the town as often as there is need, and each conveying is worth 2d. And he has to cart firewood to the courtyard against the lord's visit, and each carting is worth 2d. And he has to come twice a year for the lord's boon-work with his oxen. And this ploughing is worth 8d if he has 8 oxen. And he has to carry the lord's victuals to Stonebridge [the bridge of Stone?], and this is worth 10d. And he has to carry the lord's wool and cheese when necessary in the same county, or to Winterbourne or to Marlborough, and this is worth 1½d.

Appendix C

VOCABULARY OF POST-CLASSICAL WORDS USED IN THE MAIN TEACHING TEXT

andwike	[elsewhere spelt "handwrk"]
apud	to [esp. with place-names]
arura	plough-service
averium	[draught-] animal
averoc	[haymaker's] perquisite
bladum	corn, grain
boveria	byre
caretta	a cart
cario, -iare	to cart
caruca	a plough
companagium	"something eaten with bread"[literally]
corigia	thong [a standard measure]
corredium	allowance, supplies
cullardus	a ram
custus	expense
gabulum	rent
garba	sheaf
grangia	granary
gula augusti	1st August [Lammas] (see p.94)
herbagium	[right of / payment for] pasturage
hibernagium	winter-sowing (see p.95)
hercio, -iare	to harrow
ivernagium	(see pp.92,95)
lardarium	larder [-rent] (see p.95)
mancus	a handle
misericordia	penalty, fine (see pp.64,95)
mullo, -onis	hay-stack
multo, -onis	sheep, wether
nona	noon
precaria	boon-service
prex	[= precaria]
quilibet	every (see p.95)
quindena	fortnight (see p.95)
serclo, -are	to hoe or weed
summagio, -iare	to transport by pack-animal
tassus	rick
terminus	term-date [e.g. Michaelmas, Lady Day]
vicinus	fellow-tenant (see pp.76,95)
virgata	yardland (see p.95)
warectum	fallow

Appendix D

Line-by-line Transcription of Text XIX

1. Rogerus clericus tenet j virgatam terre et solvit de gabulo per annum vj s. ad iiij terminos
2. anni et de dono ad lardarium xj d. et debet lavare et tondere oves domini cum aliis
3. vicinis suis et valet hoc ij d. et debet arare domino pro unoquoque iugo boum quod habuerit in
4. proximis xv diebus ante Nativitatem Beati Johannis et in proximis xv sequentibus unam acram
5. ad warettum et tantumdem debet arare domino in quindena proxima ante Festum Sancti Martini et in
6. quindena proxima sequenti, et valet arura iiij boum xiiij d. Et debet ire ad granarium domini cum
7. sacco suo et equo et inde ducere semen ad acram domini quam araverit et eandem acram
8. herciare et valet j d. et dominus inveniet seminatorem. Et pro hoc waretto et hac arura
9. et herciatura habebit iiij averia cum bobus domini in pastura quieta de herbagio, et si
10. plura averia habuerit quam iiij dabit pro unoquoque quod duos dentes habuerit ij den.
11. ad Gulam Augusti et ad Festum Sancti Andree iij d. et pro quolibet quod dentem non habuerit
12. j d. ad Gulam Augusti et ad Festum Sancti Andree j d.ob. Et debet falcare pratum
13. domini per vj dies de consuetudine in Suthmede et valet vj d. Et habebit quolibet
14. die suum averoc, scilicet tantum herbe quantum poterit levare cum manco falcis sue
15. sicut pertinet ad averoc, et mancus non tanget terram. Et si mancus in illa herba levan-
16. da frangatur, perdet herbam et nulla alia misericordia pertinet. Et totum debent[1] spargere herbam
17. et ferre aquam ad falces acuendas. Et habebit illum caseum qui factus fuerit in curia domini ultimo die
18. sex predictorum dierum quibus debet falcare et secundum meliorem cullardum in falda domini cum vicinis
19. suis. Et si dominus nullum cullardum vel multonem in falda sua haberet, habebit predicto die
20. pro ipso cullardo cum vicinis suis xij d. Et debet falcare per iij dies ad precarias in
21. Westmede et nichil habere et valet vj d., et debet levare pratum et valet v d., et cariare fenum
22. et valet iij d. et facere mullonem et valet ob. Et debet serclare cum j homine post nonam per j
23. diem et valet quadrans. Et debet metere quolibet die in autumpno dimidiam acram dum bladum domini fuerit
24. metendum preter diem sabbati, et habere unam garbam per corigiam, et valet messio x d,
25. et per duos dies in autumpno unam acram integram, et habere duas garbas quolibet die,
26. et valet messio ij d. Et debet cariare bladum domini quam diu fuerit cariandum et quando ca-
27. riat, non debet metere, et quando metit, non debet cariare. Et quando cariat tota die [sic] habe-
28. bit duas garbas sero meliores in ultima caretta quam cariaverit. Et si per dimidiam
29. diem, j garbam, et valet cariacio xij d. Et debet invenire ij homines ad ij precarias domini
30. in autumpno, scilicet ad utramque duos, et debent bis comedere ad custum domini in pane, cer-
31. visio et companagio, et valet messio iiij d. Et debet venire ad precarias domini cum caru-
32. ca sua de consuetudine semel in anno ad yvernagium et herciare cum equo suo quan-
33. tum arat, et dominus pascet illum et herciatorem suum semel in die in pane, cervisio et
34. companagio. Et debet summagiare ter in anno apud Glaston', scilicet qualibet vice dimidium
35. quarterium, et qualibet vice habere de dono domini cum vicinis suis ij d., scilicet ipse et omnes qui
36. summagiant. Et valet summagiacio xvij d. Et si grangia domini vel boveria fu-
37. erit impleta stramine, adiuvabit cum j homine ad illas deliberandas, et valet ob.
38. Et si in grangia domini fuerit bladum et debeat extrahi et inde fieri tassus, debet cum j
39. homine adiuvare ad precarias et non de consuetudine. Et debet cariare corredium domini....

---

1. <u>recte</u>, **totam**(herbam) **debet** [sing.].

Appendix E

COMMENTS ON THE SCRIBAL HAND USED IN TEXT XX

IN GENERAL.

Compared with our principal text, this new text appears to be in a cursive hand, less formal, more rounded, the minims being less vertical. At the same time this hand has flourishes attached to several letters that did not have them in Text VI. Nevertheless, as I have admitted, there are resemblances between the two hands.

IN PARTICULAR.

b, **h**, and **l** are conspicuously alike in having the top split like a green twig that has been clumsily broken in half, the ends turning away in either direction, though the pattern is not symmetrical.

d is altogether different in construction from the one we met previously. Probably our other **d** was made in two strokes, first the c-like bowl, and then the "ascender" in fact planing <u>down</u> to meet the bowl. Our new **d** is judged by Johnson and Jenkinson to have been made in a continuous line, the "c" being "continued upwards and turned over to form the down-stroke which closes the letter. The oblique down-stroke is strongly marked." In fact it is this thickened inner line that first catches the eye, in my opinion. Often the scribe has pressed so heavily that the ink has spread to fill the gap between the thin upwards line and the "strongly marked" downwards line.

c and **t** are perhaps less easily distinguished in this hand, though the **t** seems to have a more resolute cross-stroke, extending to the left of its meeting-point with the curve **(t)**, **u** and **n** are often clearly identifiable, but minims still present problems. Thus in line 6 there is not a lot of difference between the number **iij** and the **m** of <u>molend</u>.

The "short" **s** (the one like the modern **s**) is often deformed, one or other of the tails touching the middle (as in solid, line 6), and it has an angular appearance . Rather in the same manner **a** and **p** have a squarish appearance . We occasionally get the **2**-like **r**, but generally the tailed **r** is found.

Some CAPITALS are familiar: the **P** in Pastura, the **E** in Ec/clesia and (with **T** and **R**) in T R E (Tempore Regis Edwardi). More troublesome are the initial letters of these words:

1.1  1.3 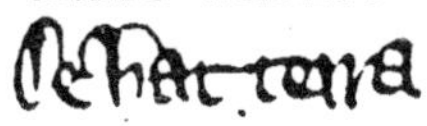 1.10  1.11 

You may not know the place-name Deverel, but **D** seems the obvious candidate for the gaps in -e hac terra and -e eadem terra.

The fourth item is made harder by being a contraction and by the disguising effect of the overlap of the double letter. The context is quite promising, but the last word on line 10 is obscure. Let me suggest that it is a suspended word, beginning hid.... We then have,

De eadem terra tenet j miles j hid... et virgatam terre de.......

"Of this same land one knight holds 1 hide and 1 virgate of land from/of......."

Of whom does he hold it? Look again at the double letter; like other double letters, its second seems to lie over the first, obscuring its right-hand edge. But the right-hand edge of the second is, after all, just visible. We have a **b**, in fact **bb**. So this contracted word includes a double **b**. Also it must be third declension as its ablative (after de) ends in -**e**. Abbas, Abbatis, **Abbate** seems likely. So the initial capital letter is **A**. And suddenly our view of it shifts and it looks like an **a**! True, a rather tall, squashed cursive **a**, with an unexpected loop top right which turns the thing into an elongated figure of 8. But we can now hope to recognise the shape again.

INDEX OF WORDS CITED FROM <u>TEXT VI</u>

The words are arranged alphabetically by letters without regard to "signs".

Numbers refer to pages of this book.

INDEX OF SUBJECTS

Certain general topics are not covered by this index, since they crop up so frequently in the book:
abbreviation/shortening
grammar
meaning and context
parallel expressions

Bold type indicates major treatment; brackets indicate pages on which the subject is implied rather than named.

Acknowledgements

My debt to the late Ronald Latham is immense. He patiently endured a barrage of pleas for help through the post in my early days of struggling with Latin manuscript. However, neither he nor any other can be held responsible for the idiosyncrasies or errors that may be detected in these pages.

I am grateful to the librarians of Trinity College, Cambridge and of the British Library for supplying microfilm copies of the manuscripts on which I have so heavily drawn. I record here my thanks to the Master and Fellows of Trinity College, Cambridge for permission to use extracts from Manuscript R.5.33, and to the British Library for permission to make use of extracts from Add.MS 17450.

I owe particular gratitude to my tame readers. Frances Davies, unofficial mentor and prop, kindly found time to read through a late draft, offering the perspective of a historian who had read many pages of medieval Latin in manuscript. My brother, Bernard Gosden, has patiently read this in its two main drafts, devoting to it his immense capacity for attending to detail. Without his help, many pages of this would have been spattered with illogical thought, clumsy English, and sheer inconsistency. My wife added the kindness of acting as third reader to her forbearance while I was in love with the Word Processor. Since then I have had the benefit of scholarly criticism from publishers' readers, most of which I have used.

My debt to published works on palaeography will be evident (see Further Reading). I also read with profit Elizabeth Thoyts' early manual, <u>How to Decipher and Study Old Documents</u> (1893).

Finally, without dropping names I can only refer anonymously to the kindness and encouragement I have had from various scholars since I took up medieval studies. I little knew what fellowship of knowledge awaited me.

Redditus et servicia villanorum.

Rogerus clericus tenet .j. virgatam terre et soluit de gablo per annum .vj. s. ad .iiij. terminos
anni. Et de dono ad lardarium .xj. d. Et debet lauare et tondere oues domini cum aliis
vicinis suis et valet hoc .ij. d. Et debet arare domino per unoquoque iugo boum quod habet in
proximis .xv. diebus ante natale beati Iohannis. et in proximis .xv. sequentibus unam acram
ad warectum. Et tantumdem debet arare domino in quindenam proxima ante festum sancti Martini et in
quindenam proxima sequenti. Et valet arura .iiij. boum .xiiij. d. Et debet ire ad granarium domini cum
sacco suo et equo et inde ducere semen ad agrum domini quem arauit. Et eandem acram
herciare et valet .j. d. Et dominus inueniet seminatorem. Et pro hoc warecto et herciatione
et herciatione habebit .iiij. animalia cum bobus domini in pastura quiete de herbagio. Et si
plura animalia habuerit quam .iiij. dabit pro unoquoque quod duos dentes habuerit .ij. denarios
ad Gulam Augusti. et ad festum sancti Andree .iij. d. Et pro quolibet quod dentem non habuerit
.j. d. ad Gulam Augusti. Et ad festum sancti Andree .j. d. ob. Et debet falcare pratum
domini per .vj. dies de consuetudine in Sithmede. Et valet .vj. d. Et habebit quolibet
die suum averoc. scilicet tantum herbe quantum poterit leuare cum manico falcis sue
sicut pratum ad averoc et manicus non tangat terram. et si manicus in illa herba leuanda
defrigatur: perdet herbam et nullam aliam mittat pratum. Et totum debent spargere herbam
et ferre acram ad falcandum acuendum. Et habebit illum caseum qui factus fuerit in curia domini ultimo die
sex predictorum dierum quibus debet falcare et secundum meliorem cullardum in falda domini cum vicinis
suis. Et si dominus nullum cullardum uel multonem in falda sua habuerit: habebit predicto die
pro ipso cullardo cum vicinis suis .xij. d. Et debet falcare per .iij. dies ad pratum in
Westmede et nichil habere. et valet .vj. d. Et debet leuare pratum et valet .v. d. et cariare fenum.
Et valet .iij. d. Et facere mullonem et valet ob. Et debet sarclare cum .j. homine post nonam per .j.
diem. Et valet quadrantem. Et debet metere quolibet die in autumpno dimidiam acram dum bladum domini fuerit
metendum preter diem sabbati et habere unam garbam per corrigiam. Et valet messio .x. d.
Et per duos dies in autumpno unam acram integram et habere duas garbas quolibet die.
et valet messio .ij. d. Et debet cariare bladum domini quamdiu fuerit cariandum. et quando ca
riat non debet metere. et quando metit non debet cariare. Et quando cariat tota die ha
bebit duas garbas scilicet meliores in ultima careta quam cariauit. Et sic per dimidiam
diem .j. garbam. Et valet cariagium .xij. d. Et debet inuenire .ij. homines ad precariam domini
in autumpno. scilicet ad utramque duos et debent bis comedere ad custum domini in pane cer
uisia et companagio. et valet messio .iiij. d. Et debet uenire ad precariam domini cum caru
ca sua de consuetudine semel in anno. ad seminagium et herciare cum equo suo quan
tum arat. et dominus pascet illum et herciatorem suum semel in die in pane ceruisia et
companagio. Et debet summagiare semel in anno apud Glaston. scilicet qualibet vice dimidium
quarterium. Et qualibet vice habere de dono domini cum vicinis suis .ij. d. scilicet ipse et omnes qui
summagiant. Et valet summagiatio .xvij. d. Et si grangia domini uel bouaria fu
erit impleta stramine: dominabit cum .j. homine ad illas deliberandas. Et valet ob.
Et si grangia domini fuerit soluta et debeat cooperiri et inde fieri tassus: debet cum .j.
homine adminiare ad precariam et non de consuetudine. Et debet cariare corredium domini

Ric' faber ten3 di. virgat' t're. et debet r'dde dno de gablo .iii. s' pann' ad .iiii. t'

tios. Si no' facit ferramenta ⁊ i' omib3 facie sic sup'dcs Walt's. Set p' gablo

no' ... ferramenta .iii. carucar'. Et soluet ad lardar' .v. d. ob. q'lib3

anno. Et d3 ferrare .ii. aff' i' pedib3 ante vt vnu' a'n' tercio de ferro dni.

Et val3 hoc .vi. d. Et d3 face de ferro dni kelt ⁊ ligamina ad carruc'

dni. Et d3 ligare vasa ad ca's dni. si fracta fuerint. Et d3 adiuuare la

uare oues dni ⁊ colligere lanam ⁊ h'ebit unu' agnu' q'lib3 anno. Et erit

ille agn' vni' anni masc'. et alt'o anno femell'. Et h'ebit q'lib3 anno .i.

nigru' vellus. ⁊ unu' cas' fem an' f'ar' sci Johis. ⁊ vnu' discu' plenu' de bu

tiro ad follos suos. ⁊ .i. aff' sup pastur' dni sn' h'bag'. Et d3 ee p' .i. die

cu' .i. hoie ad mullone' feni ⁊ ad tassum bladi simil'r. Et d3 inuenire .ii. hoies

ad p'car' autumpni sic vn' virgat'. et d3 h're .ii. a'ia cu' bob3 dni i' pastu'

q'cta de h'bagio. q' si iunga' arabit q'ntu' vn' virgat' p' iugo suo Et si pla'

fuerit faciet ip'e sic d'cs Rog's cl'icus.

Rog's de ponte t3 .v. acr' t're. et redd3 inde de gablo pann' .ii. s'. ad .iiii. t'ios ⁊ iii d' ob ⁊ teall'

Et tn' erit quiet' ab o'i op'e usq3 ad Gulam Aug'ti. Et p' Gulam ob ad lard'

aug'ti. metere d3 ⁊ opari quolib3 die ⁊ val' opacio .ii. d'. Et si sit opari' faciet o'ia anno .iii. gall'

subscripta ⁊ valent .vi. s'. iii. d. ⁊ ip'e ⁊ duo alii vicini sui de eade' tenura ⁊ galli. Alias

... soluent p' annu' de dono ad lardar' .xi. d. Et si sit opar' d3 opari p' tres dies .iii. gall' ⁊ .i. ...

16 i' septima' nisi festa i'tuenia't ~~scil. die lune, die mart' ⁊ die veneris~~. Et si i' festo sci Mich...

d3 trit'are t'rabit .ii. bus' fr'i ut ordi ⁊ ventare. Et de auen' vl' dragg' .iiii. b'.

cumulatos ⁊ h'ebit. Et si no' ~~triturare~~ fossabit ut cooperiet ut aliq'd aliud op'

faciet usq3 ad horam t'tiam. Et si d3 fossare fossabit i' plena t'ra .xv. pe

des. Et i' veteri fossato erigendo .xxx. pedes. Et a Gula Aug'ti us3 ad festu' sci Mi

chael' d3 cotidie opari siue metere siue aliud op' q'd ei destinatu' fuit face.

Et si metit debet metere di. acr' ⁊ h're garbam p' congia' sicut p'dcs Rog's

cl'icus. Et q'ndocu'q3 dns aduenit t'rabit p'bendam suam q'lib3 die adue

nit. Et si fuerit carucari' ip'e ⁊ soci' suus h'ebunt vna' de caruc' dni p'

duos dies sabb'i q'tinuos. ⁊ dns p' .i. diem sabb'i ⁊ hoc p' tot' annu'. Et si sit

bercari' dni h'ebit .i. agnu' ⁊ .i. vell' ⁊ falda' dni sup t'ram sua' p' .xii.

dies ad Nat'. Et h'ebit vnam de caruc' dni quotiens vn' carucar'. Et

h'ebit .xv. oui' i' fald' dni. Et si sint matres oui' h'ebit lac eard'. Et habe

bit suu' me'ge sic vna festa q' tradit ad faldam. Et canis suus h'ebit ab

hocked' us3 ad Gulam Aug'ti quolib3 die unu' plenu' cifu' plenu' de m'ge.

p'mu' supt'u'. Et dabit ad chyrsurt die sci Martini vno anno scil. q'n camp'

orientalis colit' .iiii. gallin' ⁊ .i. gall'. et alt'o anno q'n camp' occidentalis colit'

.iii. gallin' ⁊ .i. gall'. si fuerit cu' vxore. ut vxor cu' viro. Et si ita fuerit

no' dabit n' medietate' Chyrsurt. Et si porc' h'uit dabit p' vno q'q3 porc'

sup annu' .i. d. Die sci Martini ad pannag' ⁊ p' porc' de di. anni. ob. Et si

Ricardus Faber tenet dimidiam virgatam terre et deberet dare de gabulo iij sol. per annum ad iiij terminos si non faceret ferramenta et in omnibus facere sicut supradictus Walterus. Set pro gabulo nunc preparabit ferramenta iiij carucarum et solvet ad lardarium v den.obol. quolibet anno. Et debet ferrare ij affros in pedibus ante vel unum ante et retro de ferro domini. Et valet hoc vj den. Et debet facere de ferro domini rellia et ligamina ad carucas domini. Et debet ligare vasa ad caseum domini si fracta fuerint. Et debet adiuvare lavare oves domini et colligere lanam, et habebit unum agnum quolibet anno. Et erit ille agnus uno[1] anno masculus et altero anno femellus. Et habebit quolibet anno j nigrum vellus et unum caseum factum ante Nativitatem sancti Johannis et unum discum plenum de butiro ad folles suos et j affrum super pasturam domini sine herbagio, et debet esse per j diem cum j homine ad mullonem feni et ad tassum bladi similiter. Et debet invenire ij homines ad precarias autumpni sicut unus virgatarius, et debet habere ij averia cum bobus domini in pastura quieta de herbagio, que si junga[sic] arabit quantum unus virgatarius pro iugo suo. Et si plura habuerit, faciet inde sicut dictus Rogerus Clericus.

Rogerus de Ponte tenet v acras terre et reddet inde de gabulo per annum ij sol.ad iiij terminos[2] [erasure here] et tunc erit quietus ab omni opere usque ad Gulam Augusti, et post Gulam Augusti metere debet et operari quolibet die et valet operacio ij sol. Et si sit operarius, faciet omnia subscripta et valent vj sol.iij d. et ipse et duo alii vicini sui de eadem tenura [3]solvent per annum de dono ad lardariumxj den. et si sit operarius debet operari per tres dies in septimana nisi festa interveniant [scilicet die lune, die mercurii et die veneris][4]. Et si debet triturare, triturabit ij bussellos frumenti vel ordei, et de avena vel draggia iiij bussellos cumulatos et nil habebit. Et si [non triturat[4]] fossabit vel cohoperiet vel aliquod aliud opus faciet usque ad horam tertiam, et si debet fossare fossabit in plena terra xv pedes, et in veteri fossato erigendo xxx pedes, et a Gulausto usque ad festum Sancti Michaelis debet cotidie operari sive metere sive aliud opus quod ei destinatum fuerit facere. Et si metit[7] debet metere dimidiam acram et habere garbam per corigiam sicut predictus Rogerus Clericus. Et quandocumque dominus advenerit triturabit prebendam suam[8] quacumque die advenerit. Et si fuerit carucarius ipse et socius suus habebunt unam de carucis domini per duos dies sabbati continuos, et dominus per tertium diem sabbati, et hoc per totum annum. Et si sit Bercarius domini habebit j agnum et j vellus et faldam domini super terram suam per xij dies ad Natale, et habebit unam de carucis domini quociens unus carucarius, et habebit xv oves in falda domini, et si sint matrices oves habebit lac earundem, et habebit suum mege sicut una femina que vadit ad faldam. Et canis suus habebit ab hockedai usque ad Gulam Augusti quolibet die unum plenum cifum plenum de mege primum sumptum. Et dabit ad chursuttum die Sancti Martini uno anno, scilicet quando campus orientalis colitur, iiij gallinas et j gallum et altero anno, quando campus campus occidentalis colitur, iij gallinas et j gallum, nisi fuerit sine uxore vel uxor sine viro. Quod si ita fuerit non dabit nisi medietatem Churisutti. Et si porcos habuerit, dabit pro unoquoque porco superannato j den. die Beati Martini ad pannagium et pro porco de dimidio anno obol. Et si

---

1. The scribe wrote uni anni, then expunged the **i**'s and wrote **o** above each.
2. In another hand in r.h.margin: iij d.ob.et tertiam partem oboli ad lardarium et ... anno iij gallinas et j gallum, alio anno iiij or gallinas et j gallum in festo Sancti Martini ad churischettum.
3. In another hand in l.h.margin: quietus tum/tam ... ij s.
4. These words crossed out (the form of 'cancelling' used for such a short piece).
5. Between lines 20 and 21, in another hand, after ordei: sine cumulo.
6. Between lines 22 and 23, in another hand, after faciet: ab ortu solis.
7. The scribe has added a superscript sign suggesting meterit, - a non-classical formation.
8. Between lines 26 and 27, in another hand, above suam, there is written very faintly what may be as follows: sive fil? ad gabulum suum (+ a line possibly linking adve to) op..ri j

Also published by Llanerch:

A BOOK OF BRITISH BALLADS
edited by Roy Palmer

BALLADS AND SONGS OF BRITTANY
Tom Taylor

BUSHED AND BRIARS
Folk Songs Collected by
Ralph Vaughan Williams
edited by Roy Palmer

BESOM MAKER
Heywood Summer

105 SONGS OF OCCUPATION FROM THE
WESTERN ISLES OF SCOTLAND
Frances Tolmie

A GARLAND OF COUNTRY SONG
Sabine Baring Gould

NORTHUMBRIAN MINSTRELSY
Bruce and Stokoe

TRADITIONAL TUNES
Frank Kidson

BROADSIDE BLACK-LETTER BALLADS
J Payne Collier

COMPLETE COLLECTION OF IRISH MUSIC
(3 volumes)
George Petrie

MANX BALLADS AND MUSIC
A W Moore

ANCIENT IRISH MUSIC
or 100 airs hitherto unpublished
collected and edited by P W Joyce